Sustainable Systems

Development and Learning

Winston W. H. Weng

Decision Analysis for
Sustainable Development
From the Aspects of
Knowledge and Education

Sustainable Systems

Development and Learning

Winston W. H. Weng

Decision Analysis for
Sustainable Development
From the Aspects of
Knowledge and Education

Sustainable Systems: Development and Learning

Contents

Preface ... Preface-1

About the author ... Author-1

Chapter 1 ... 1-1

Sustainable Systems Architecture

Chapter 2 ... 2-1

Sustainable Systems Development

Chapter 3 ... 3-1

Sustainable Systems Education and Learning

Preface

A sustainable system has two meanings: sustainability within the system and sustainability through the system. This book presents three key aspects of sustainable systems: system architecture, system development, and system education and learning.

Chapter 1 examines the critical components that influence the sustainability of IoT-enabled smart systems. It constructs a layered modular architecture framework for sustainable systems, which is evaluated using the Decision-Making Trial and Evaluation Laboratory (DEMATEL) method, based on empirical data collected from experts.

Chapter 2 identifies the factors that impact the sustainability of the smart systems development lifecycle. Given that the development and maintenance of sustainable systems are highly knowledge-intensive, the knowledge-based view is employed as the theoretical foundation for identifying the critical factors in the decision-making process of sustainable systems development.

Chapter 3 presents a qualitative case study on education and learning related to sustainable systems. It explores the interrelationships among education programs, learning processes, students, IT professionals, and the sustainable development of societies, particularly in the context of the impacts of COVID-19 outbreaks.

The theme of this book aligns closely with several of the United Nations Sustainable Development Goals (SDGs) for 2030, particularly SDG 4 (Quality Education), SDG 8 (Decent Work and Economic Growth), SDG 9 (Industry, Innovation, and Infrastructure), and SDG 11 (Sustainable Cities and Communities).

I hope you enjoy reading this book.

Sustainable Systems: Development and Learning

About the author

Winston W. H. Weng is an independent researcher and writer. His research focuses on the sustainable development of the IT software industry. He has participated in a large number of research projects involving topics such as enterprise IT investments, IT outsourcing, business software, embedded software, open-source software, IT security, technology services, and the e-development of industries. Previously, he was a project manager working on topics including IT system development and maintenance services. He was also responsible for consultancy and training services for the e-development of corporations.

Chapter 1
Sustainable Systems Architecture

Abstract

The IoT-enabled smart systems provide great convenience to users but also raise issues about sustainability impacts. So far, studies of the sustainability in IoT-enabled smart systems are relatively scant. This research thus examines critical components which influence the sustainability of IoT-enabled smart systems. An empirical study was performed using DEMATEL method with data collected from industry experts. The results conclude a cause and effect relationship of the factors influencing smart system sustainability. The study discovered that the components in the network and big data aspects are of the highest priority for sustainability improvement and each of the evaluation aspects and components identify the necessary precaution for the sustainability in an IoT-enabled smart system.

Keywords: Internet of Things; sustainability; smart system; DEMATEL

1. Introduction

Recent development of the extensive pandemic, the meticulousness of enterprise internationalization and business integration, and the rapid development of innovative technologies have caused business environments to change rapidly and enormously. For enterprises, customers require an increasingly fast response and personalized fulfillment. To respond effectively to changing internal situations and external environments, firms develop smart systems using smart technologies such as the Internet of Things (IoT) (Gubbi, Buyya, Marusic, & Palaniswami, 2013; Porter & Heppelmann, 2015). A firm must interact closely with customers through its distinctive system capabilities to achieve a sustainable competitive advantage (Weng, 2020b). This makes IoT-enabled smart systems especially critical for firms facing economic, environmental, and societal challenges (Braccini & Margherita, 2019). In an era of rapid product lifecycles with emergent information technologies such as big data analytics (Weng, 2020a), cloud computing (Wu, Lan, & Lee, 2011), and smart mobile devices (Porter & Heppelmann, 2015; Weng, 2020b), IoT-enabled smart systems become even more critical for enterprises.

IoT-enabled smart systems are developed with multiple purposes in enterprise operations (Porter & Heppelmann, 2015). Nevertheless, as the concept of sustainability emerges, the development and use of smart systems are required to be aligned with the goal of corporate sustainability. However, determining the factors influencing the sustainability of smart systems is complex, and research in this regard is rare so far. The goal of this paper is to fill this gap by proposing a systematic process to analyze critical factors which affect the sustainability of IoT-enabled smart systems.

The paper begins with a review of the relevant literature about sustainability, the Internet of Things, and smart systems. Then it proposes a decisional framework which assesses critical components for achieving sustainability of IoT-enabled smart systems. Following that, the framework is evaluated with the decision-making trial and evaluation laboratory (DEMATEL) method using empirical data collected from experts. Finally, the findings are presented along with managerial implications of the study, its limitations and recommendations for future work.

2. Materials and Methods
2.1. Theoretical Background
2.1.1. IoT-enabled Smart Systems

The layered modular architecture framework (Yoo, Henfridsson, & Lyytinen, 2010) is widely studied for analyzing innovative digital systems. The involvement of contemporary digital technology is partitioned into device, network, service, and content in the framework. In the context of the framework, an IoT-enabled smart system is an integrated architecture with various hardware and software components (Porter & Heppelmann, 2015; Weng, 2020b). Among its major features, ubiquitous sensing enabled by wireless sensor network is the mechanism that the "things" in the IoT perform surveillance on the surrounding physical environment, detect and record the changes, and respond to the changes with adaptive learning (Baucas & Spachos, 2020; Pal & Kant, 2018). IoT contains multiple layers of communication networking infrastructure to provide the collaboration between people and people, people and things, and things and things, to form a converged environment (Atzori, Iera, & Morabito, 2010; Gubbi et al., 2013). Big data in IoT-enabled smart systems are processed through embedded computing functionality. IoT devices contain embedded hardware and software to work intelligently within the cyber-physical converged environment.

  The IoT enables the realization of many smart devices for personal, business and public applications

(Braccini & Margherita, 2019; Gubbi et al., 2013). For a firm with IoT capability, large scale real-time customer surveys can be conducted with the assistance of sensing and recognition technology. IoT-enabled smart systems can also assist the collection and dissemination of user opinions and user experiences about products or services (Gubbi et al., 2013). Moreover, the ubiquitous sensing with intelligent pattern recognition and machine-learning functionalities enables the personalization and customization of new products and services. Therefore, an IoT-enabled smart system is functionalized with interaction among components of network, big data, service, and device.

IoT-enabled smart systems contain embedded hardware and software to work intelligently within the surrounding. The embedded hardware includes processor chips, data storage units, and power units. The embedded software includes embedded operating systems, mobile apps, and middleware. In particular, IoT devices can be embedded further in other devices (Gubbi et al., 2013; Krotov, 2017). IoT monitored and detected information is invisibly embedded in the environment around users, results in the generation of big data in real-time, which is distributed, stored, processed, presented, and interpreted in a seamless, efficient, and easily understandable form (Gubbi et al., 2013; Krotov, 2017). Cloud support is provided by IoT systems for processing the real-time analytics. IoT systems deploy cloud services to assist the processing and storage of IoT analytics, and provide IoT users ubiquitous access to supporting services initiated by IoT devices around the smart environment (Atzori et al., 2010; Bradley et al., 2015; Gubbi et al., 2013). Users of the IoT-enabled smart systems are supported with interactive user interface tools. Visualizing, touching, and listening are critical for an IoT-enabled smart system as these functions allow the system users to be aware of the changes in the surrounding. 3D viewing and printing technologies, personal mobile assistants, wearable devices, and augmented-reality systems provide a novel interface for users to interact with the converged environment (Bradley et al., 2015; Gubbi et al., 2013). Integrating the IoT with the recent development of the blockchain technology is the next major challenge to expand the applications of the IoT-enabled smart systems (Huh, Cho, & Kim, 2017; Khan & Salah, 2018; Novo, 2018; Reyna, Martín, Chen, Soler, & Díaz, 2018).

Furthermore, the IoT technologies are commercialized by embedding IoT components in various interconnected smart products. IoT enables the evolution of various products such as smart home appliances, robots, drones, crewless cars, automated factory machines and business equipment, and many other innovative devices (Krotov, 2017; Miorandi, Sicari, De Pellegrini, & Chlamtac, 2012; Porter & Heppelmann, 2015; Weng & Lin, 2014, 2015). The smart environments and interconnected smart products can further enable cyber-physical convergence. The convergence of computer networks, telecom networks, and the IoT triggers further convergence of cyberspace and physical space, and results in various smart spaces, such as smart home, smart office, smart factory, smart laboratory, smart store, smart marketplace, smart hospital, smart museum, and smart city (Agarwal & Brem, 2015; Bradley et al., 2015; Gubbi et al., 2013; Miorandi et al., 2012).

2.1.2. Sustainability for Smart Systems

Firms worldwide require maintaining sustainable production and managerial response to changing environments to sustain competitive advantage. Such a response requires a firm to indicate the sustainable performance on overall business process to achieve the firm's goal of financial performance, social responsibility, and waste elimination to reduce the impact to the environment (Hammer & Pivo, 2017). Sustainability is important for the firm's continuous improvement in the environment with great emphasis on green product development in a competitive and sustainable market. The major cause for the continued deterioration of the global environment is the unsustainable pattern of consumption and production, especially in highly industrialized societies.

However, sustainability is still a complex concept (Chiu, Chang, Chen, Chiou, & Chang, 2016). There is a growing consensus that sustainability is necessary to move towards developing performance measures for promoting and evaluating achievements. Many companies are beginning to understand the importance of sustainable development of their products and services, although they are not certain how the concept applies to their business activities. Consequently, firms must integrate their resources and sustainability to ensure corporate survival. Sustainability engenders multi-dimensional difficulties that involve numerous organizational aspects and integration among various aspects. The sustainable performances of a smart system have seldom been determined because the social and environmental activities are inherent and have high uncertainty and imprecision for assessment. The sustainable performance indicators are uncertain and unpredictable, and difficult to assess accurately (Su et al., 2016).

Previous studies suggested that sustainability be measured with the triple bottom line (TBL): economical, environmental, and social performances (Braccini & Margherita, 2019). A firm's performances in these three dimensions need to be well balanced. Sustainability has become a critical objective in the entire life cycle of the design, development, and maintenance of corporate products and services (Chiu et al., 2016). However, the studies in the sustainability perspective are still rare for smart systems.

In the development of smart systems, factors influencing the performances in these three dimensions of the TBL need to be considered simultaneously

(Venters et al., 2018). These factors often interact and affect each other. For example, a malfunction of sensing may cause errors in object detection and recognition for surveillance services. Bugs in big data analytics and machine learning software component could jeopardize the accuracy of collaboration services, and fail the entire smart systems. Therefore, the key factors that are influential in determining the overall system sustainability need to be identified, and the cause and effect relationships among these factors need to be clarified. Thus, determining the critical components for the sustainability of an IoT-enabled smart system is a multiple criteria decision-making (MCDM) problem (Si, You, Liu, & Zhang, 2018; Tang, Tzeng, & Wang, 1999; Wu et al., 2011).

2.2. DEMATEL Method

The decision making trial and evaluation laboratory (DEMATEL) method is an MCDM techniques with applications in various areas (Lin, Yang, Kang, & Yu, 2011; Wu et al., 2011). The DEMATEL method not only deliver a means to visualize the causal relationships among criteria through a cause-effect diagram, but also evaluates the intensity to which the factors influence each other (Si et al., 2018). Thus it is suitable for the purpose of this study.

The conventional DEMATEL (Fontela & Gabus, 1976; Si et al., 2018) method contains four major steps: generating an initial direct relation matrix, normalizing the direct relation matrix, calculating the total relation matrix, and drawing the causal diagram (Si et al., 2018; Wu et al., 2011). In general, the major steps of the DEMATEL can be described as follows.

1. The direct relation matrix

The intensity of the relationship between criteria i and j is expressed by the comparison scale constructed according to the following five levels of influence: 0 for no influence, 1 for low influence, 2 for medium influence, 3 for high influence, and 4 for very high influence.

The initial direct relation matrix F is an n×n matrix that represents the pair-wise comparisons of influences and directions between criteria, in which f_{ij} represents the intensity to which criterion i affects criterion j and all principal diagonal elements are equal to zero.

$$F = [f_{ij}]_{n \times n} \quad (1)$$

2. The normalized relation matrix

The normalized direct relation matrix $Y = [y_{ij}]$ with $0 \leq y_{ij} \leq 1$ can be calculated through equations (2) and (3) as follows.

$$Y = h \times F \quad (2)$$

where

$$h = \frac{1}{max_{\ 1 \leq i \leq n} \sum_{j=1}^{n} f_{ij}} \quad (3)$$

3. The total relation matrix

After the normalized direct relation matrix Y is calculated, the total relation matrix T can be computed by using equation (4), in which I is the n×n identity matrix and $(I - Y)^{-1}$ denotes the inversion matrix of I − Y.

$$T = Y \times (I - Y)^{-1} \qquad (4)$$

4. The causal diagram

Using equations (5)–(7), the sum of rows vector and the sum of columns vector can be separately computed.

$$T = [t_{ij}]_{n \times n}, \quad i, j = 1, 2, \ldots, n \qquad (5)$$
$$r = [\textstyle\sum_{j=1}^{n} t_{ij}]_{n \times 1} \qquad (6)$$
$$c = [\textstyle\sum_{i=1}^{n} t_{ij}]_{1 \times n} \qquad (7)$$

In equations (6)–(7), vector r and vector c are the sum of rows and the sum of columns of the total relation matrix T, respectively. A causal diagram can be drawn then by mapping the elements of (r + c, r - c) to a two-dimensional graph, where the horizontal axis (r + c) is obtained by adding c to r, and the vertical axis (r - c) is obtained by subtracting c from r. A criterion belongs to the cause group if (r - c) is positive, while it belongs to the effect group if (r - c) is negative (Fontela & Gabus, 1976; Wu et al., 2011).

2.3. The Decision Process

This study conducted literature review and industry expert interviews to collect the possible factors for sustainable smart systems. The decisional factors proposed by the experts and supported by the literature encompass the triple bottom line (Braccini & Margherita, 2019) and are categorized using the layered modular architecture framework (Yoo et al., 2010) as in Table 1. The four layers include the network layer (A1), the big data layer (A2), the service layer (A3), and the device layer (A4).

The experts were then asked to rate the influence of each factor by using equation (0) described above. The final results were obtained using equations (1)-(6). The meaning and significance of these decision factors are explained as follows.

Table 1. The IoT components for smart system sustainability.

Aspect		Key IoT Component
A1 Network	P01	Wireless sensing
	P02	Seamless streaming
	P03	Cloud connectivity
A2 Big data	P04	Real-time mining
	P05	Embedded analytics
	P06	Adaptive learning
A3 Service	P07	Collaboration
	P08	Surveillance
	P09	Customization
A4 Device	P10	Public facility
	P11	Personal auxiliary
	P12	Business machinery

2.3.1. The Network Aspect

This is the mechanism that the "things" or devices in IoT perceive the surrounding physical environment, detect and record the changes in the environment, and respond to the changes. Ubiquitous sensing is enabled by wireless sensor network (WSN) technologies (Borgia, 2014; Bradley et al., 2015; Gubbi et al., 2013). IoT contains multiple layers of communication networking infrastructure to provide the pervasive communications for people to people (P2P), people to things (P2T), things to people (T2P), and things to things(T2T), and form a smart mutual communication environment (Atzori et al., 2010; Gubbi et al., 2013). Furthermore, IoT-enabled smart systems deploy cloud services to assist the processing and storage of real-time analytics, and provide system users ubiquitous access to supporting services initiated by smart devices around the smart environment (Atzori et al., 2010; Bradley et al., 2015; Gubbi et al., 2013). Cloud support for things also enables the expansion of computing and storage capacity of the IoT-enabled smart systems.

The components in the network aspect of IoT-enabled smart systems enable the efficient sensing and transmission of information. They form the digital infrastructure which empowers the interconnection of things. Thus their functionality has critical impacts on the sustainability of systems.

2.3.2. The Big Data Aspect

Data in IoT-enabled smart systems are processed with real-time streaming by embedded hardware and software in things to work intelligently within the environment. The embedded hardware includes processor chips, data storage units, and power units. The embedded software includes embedded operating systems, mobile apps, and middleware. In particular, things can be embedded further into other things. This embedded architecture enables mining streaming data in real-time (Gubbi et al., 2013; Krotov, 2017). The monitored and detected information is embedded in the devices around users, results in the generation of big data in real-time, which is distributed, stored, processed, presented, and interpreted in a seamless, efficient, and easily understandable form (Gubbi et al., 2013; Krotov, 2017). The big data from IoT connected products provide a clear picture of product use, showing the features users prefer. By comparing usage patterns, firms can identify more precise market segmentation information (Porter & Heppelmann, 2015). Moreover, the pervasive sensing and networking enable IoT devices to learn from the environment anytime and anywhere. The learning capability concerns a firm's ability to learn about customers, competitors, channel members, and the broader market environment in which it operates (Day, 1994; Morgan, Slotegraaf, & Vorhies, 2009). Using IoT can enhance intelligent learning capability because IoT capability enables a firm with a better ability to sense and collect information from customers and competitors (Yu, Nguyen, & Chen, 2016).

Thus, the components in the big data aspect support the mining, analytics, and learning capabilities of IoT-enabled smart systems. Deficiency in these components may cause system failure, generate waste, and endanger the user societies.

2.3.3. The Service Aspect

Use of IoT facilitates collaborations between firms and business partners. Information sharing in the IoT can occur among people, among people and things, and among things. Firms with IoT capability are more convenient to form virtual alliances or virtual groups with partners. These partners could be customers, suppliers, intermediaries, governments, and competitors, all of which are important in the IoT context (Yu et al., 2016). Sensing a predefined incident is often the beginning for information sharing. Information sharing can enhance situational awareness and support collaboration (Lee & Lee, 2015).

Surveillance of resource is a generic service widely utilized in system status monitoring such as human resource, inventory control, water quality, and energy preservation. IoT capability makes extensive use of artificial intelligence, simulation, automation, robotics, sensors, data collection systems, and networks towards advanced engineering and precision machining. These technologies make possible the establishment of efficient, collaborative, and sustainable smart meters and sensor grids to achieve real-time resource surveillance (Benias & Markopoulos, 2017).

Sensor-based information collected through IoT embedded products covers actions of customer purchase and use, and can be analyzed to obtain a much more precise and complete picture of the customer's characteristics and preferences (Ng, Scharf, Pogrebna, & Maull, 2015). Customer feedbacks are collected and transmitted in real-time through various sensor networks and supportive cloud services for further refinement of innovation or customization. Thus IoT capability could expand opportunities for product or service customization.

The components in the service aspect of IoT-enabled smart systems enable monitoring resource usage, identifying user preferences, and facilitating collaboration. They are thus widely utilized in applications such as smart grid, smart factory, smart inventory, and smart retail.

2.3.4. The Device Aspect

The cyber-physical convergence of computer network, telecom network, social network, and the IoT triggers further convergence of cyberspace and physical space, and results in various smart public facilities, such as smart station, smart marketplace, smart hospital, smart museum, and smart city (Agarwal & Brem, 2015;

Bradley et al., 2015; Gubbi et al., 2013; Jin, Gubbi, Marusic, & Palaniswami, 2014; Miorandi et al., 2012). Users interact with the smart public facilities through innovative interface technologies by visualizing, touching, voicing, and listening. These facilities need to be sustainable and reliable for users.

The IoT also enables the evolution and convergence of various interconnected smart personal products such as smart home appliances, home service robots, drones, crewless cars, and many other innovative devices (Krotov, 2017; Miorandi et al., 2012; Porter & Heppelmann, 2015). User interface tools such as 3D viewers and printers, personal mobile assistants, wearable devices, and augmented-reality systems provide novel media for users to interact with these smart personal auxiliaries (Bradley et al., 2015; Gubbi et al., 2013). Moreover, the IoT are also employed in automating various business domain operation machinery in manufacturing, supply chain (Cheng, Tao,

Xu, & Zhao, 2018), marketing (Lo & Campos, 2018), retail (Balaji & Roy, 2017), healthcare (Zhou & Piramuthu, 2018), and tourism (Eskerod, Hollensen, Morales-Contreras, & Arteaga-Ortiz, 2019).

All these applications require rigorous dependability and security to protect people and organizations involved. Thus sustainability is a mandatory prerequisite of the device aspect (Weber, 2010; Weinberg, Milne, Andonova, & Hajjat, 2015).

3. Results

The collected pairwise comparison of components in Table 1 were obtained (the comparison mechanism has been described at step 1 of the research method of section 2.2), and that the preliminary average direct relation matrix is shown in Tables 2-6. Based on the direct relation matrix, these numbers are normalized continuously into the normalized relation matrix (calculated by equations (2) and (3)). The total relation matrix is then obtained by using equation (4).

Finally, equations (5)-(7) have been used to produce the causal diagram by mapping a dataset of (r + c, r - c), as displayed in Tables 7 and Figures 1-5.

3.1. The Initial Direct Relation Matrices

Tables 2–6 exhibit the initial direct relation matrices of the critical factors and the four aspects. These data were obtained by taking arithmetic means of the expert assessments of the impacts of a factor on the other factors.

Table 2. Direct relation matrix of network aspect.

	P01	P02	P03
P01	0.000	2.286	1.286
P02	3.286	0.000	4.000
P03	2.714	3.286	0.000

Table 3. Direct relation matrix of big data aspect.

	P04	P05	P06
P04	0.000	3.286	2.571
P05	0.857	0.000	3.714
P06	1.857	2.714	0.000

Table 4. Direct relation matrix of service aspect.

	P07	P08	P09
P07	0.000	1.143	2.286
P08	2.143	0.000	1.286
P09	2.857	1.286	0.000

Table 5. Direct relation matrix of device aspect.

	P10	P11	P12
P10	0.000	2.143	3.286
P11	2.286	0.000	3.429
P12	1.857	1.000	0.000

Table 6. Direct relation matrix of the four aspects.

	A1	A2	A3	A4
A1	0.000	1.857	3.143	3.714
A2	0.857	0.000	3.857	3.000
A3	1.143	2.286	0.000	2.286
A4	0.143	1.429	2.571	0.000

3.2. The Total Relation Matrices

The direct relation matrices were normalized continuously into the normalized relation matrices by using equations (2) and (3). The total relation matrix is then obtained by using equation (4). The results are shown in Tables 7-11.

Table 7. Total relation matrix of network aspect.

	P01	P02	P03
P01	0.690	0.884	0.783
P02	1.473	1.099	1.412

P03	1.294	1.276	0.929

Table 8. Total relation matrix of big data aspect.

	P04	P05	P06
P04	0.703	1.599	1.642
P05	0.711	1.010	1.479
P06	0.810	1.341	1.124

Table 9. Total relation matrix of service aspect.

	P07	P08	P09
P07	0.903	0.705	1.051
P08	1.173	0.505	0.923
P09	1.389	0.790	0.838

Table 10. Total relation matrix of device aspect.

	P10	P11	P12
P10	0.51	0.64	1.07
P11	0.79	0.42	1.11
P12	0.54	0.39	0.46

Table 11. Total relation matrix of the four aspects.

	A1	A2	A3	A4
A1	0.158	0.542	0.817	0.814
A2	0.226	0.340	0.802	0.699
A3	0.219	0.464	0.411	0.567
A4	0.110	0.333	0.511	0.269

3.3. The Cause and Effect Relations

After the total relation matrices were obtained by using equation (4), equations (5)-(7) were employed to compute the cause and effect relations. The results are shown in Table 12.

Table 12. Cause and effect relation.

	r	c	r + c	r - c
P01	2.357	3.457	5.814	-1.100
P02	3.984	3.258	7.242	0.726
P03	3.498	3.124	6.623	0.374
P04	3.944	2.224	6.168	1.720
P05	3.200	3.950	7.150	-0.750
P06	3.274	4.244	7.518	-0.970
P07	2.660	3.465	6.125	-0.805
P08	2.601	2.001	4.602	0.601
P09	3.017	2.813	5.830	0.205
P10	2.226	1.841	4.067	0.386
P11	2.317	1.449	3.766	0.868
P12	1.386	2.641	4.027	-1.254

A1	2.332	0.713	3.045	1.619
A2	2.068	1.678	3.746	0.389
A3	1.661	2.542	4.203	-0.880
A4	1.223	2.350	3.573	-1.127

3.4. The Causal Diagram

Finally, the causal diagram is produced and displayed in Figure 1 by mapping the dataset of $(r + c, r - c)$ in Tables 12. Based on the data set shown in Table 12, we obtained the center panel of Figure 1, which demonstrates the causal relationships among the four aspects. The other four panels of Figure 1 demonstrate the causal relationships among the components within the aspects of network (upper left panel), big data (upper right panel), service (lower right panel), and device (lower left panel), respectively.

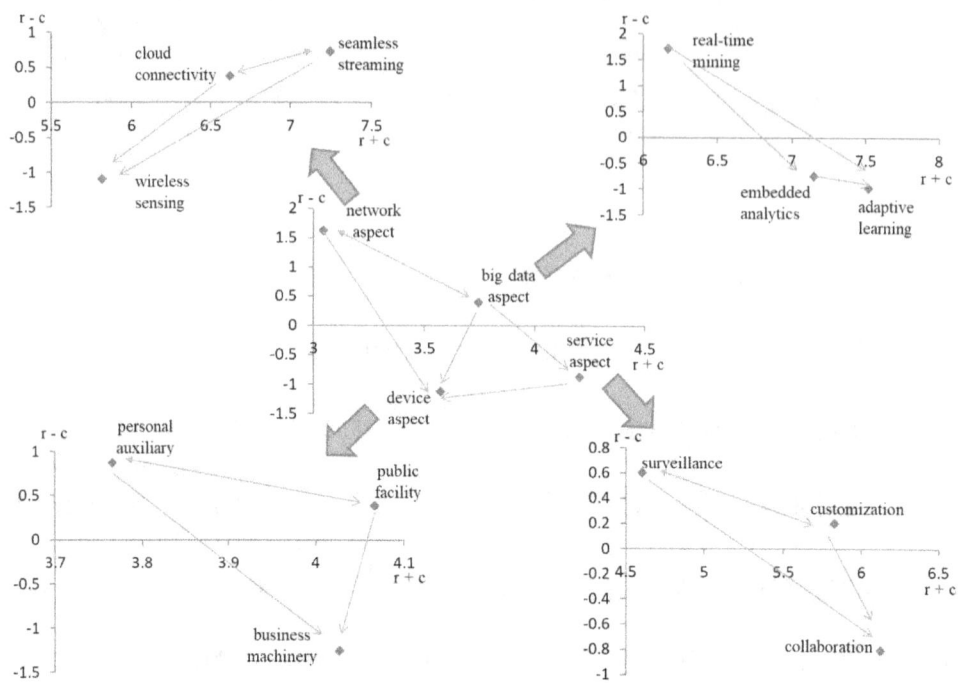

Figure 1. Causal diagram for the sustainability of IoT-enabled smart systems.

4. Discussion

Examining Figure 1 and Table 12, each factor can be analyzed, and its impact on the overall sustainability discussed. Hence, the critical components influencing the sustainability of IoT-enabled smart systems can be determined, as is discussed next.

4.1. Analysis of the Cause Factors

Since these causal factors have a net impact on the overall framework, their performance can greatly influence the overall goal. Thus, it is generally accepted that factors in the cause group should be accorded more scrutiny. However, this paper explicitly analyses each factor in the cause group to determine those that are more likely to be critical factors.

Among the factors in the cause group, the network layer (A1) has the highest $(r-c)$ value, which means that it has a greater impact on the entire framework than it receives from other factors. Further, Table 12 shows that the degree of its influential impact (r) is 2.332, ranking first among all causal factors. This indicates that it has a remarkable impact on other factors, and that its improvement can lead to the enhancement of the entire framework. Therefore, to enhance the sustainability of IoT-enabled smart systems, a reasonable cause-effect structure that can clearly define the responsibilities for decision makers should first be constructed. To summarize, the network layer is a critical factor that deserves greater attention in the overall sustainability of IoT-enabled smart systems.

The net effect score, $(r - c)$, of the big data layer (A2), which is the other cause factor, ranks second among all causal factors, and its influential impact index score ($r = 2.068$) is also the second highest of all layers. The impact that the big data has on the entire framework is significant, and its improvement will clearly enhance the effectiveness and efficiency of the system sustainability. Therefore, the results of this study suggest that the big data layer is a critical factor for the sustainability of IoT-enabled smart systems.

4.2. Analysis of the Effect Factors

Generally, the factors in the effect group tend to be easily affected by others, which make them unsuitable as critical impact factors. Nevertheless, it is necessary to discuss these factors to identify the features of each one. Thus, after further analysis, one of the two effect factors is recognized as a critical factor.

Among the effect factors, the device layer (A4) has an (r + c) score as high as 3.573, ranking third among the factors, as shown in Table 12. However, its (r − c) value is −1.127, indicating that it is easily affected by other factors. Further, analysis reveals that the degree of influential impact of the device layer is low, and the c value 2.350 is much greater than that of r.

All of the indices suggest that the device layer has a low impact on the overall framework, but is also susceptible to other factors, and that an adjustment of the other factors can lead to an improvement in the sustainability of the device layer; therefore, this layer is clearly not a cause factor.

As shown in Figure 1, it is evident that the service layer (A3) is an effect factor with an (r − c) value of −0.880 (see Table 12), which is below zero. This result suggests that the service layer is subject to a net effect from other factors, and that it concurrently has a considerable impact on the framework. However, Table 12 reveals that the service layer has an (r + c) score as high as 4.203, ranking first among all four layers. In addition, an improvement of the service layer can be easily achieved by enhancing other layers. Therefore, this layer is recognized as a critical factor.

4.3. Analysis of the Critical Factors within the Four Aspects

4.3.1. The Network Layer

As shown in the IoT infrastructure panel of Figure 2 and Table 5, seamless streaming is more influential than cloud connectivity, as indicated by the higher (r − c) value, and also has a direct influence on wireless sensing. It is also the most important component in the networking aspect with the highest (r + c) value.

Thus, with respect to the network aspect, seamless streaming is the most influential component and should be improved and promoted first, followed by cloud connectivity and wireless sensing, as shown in Fig.1. Seamless streaming can enhance the stability and quality of data transmission in the system and reduce system failure and human error, thus it has positive economic and social impact.

4.3.2. The Big Data Layer

In the big data panel of Figure 2, real-time mining had the greatest (r − c) value, 1.720, which directly affected the embedded analytics and adaptive learning. Therefore, real-time mining is the most essential component, since it affects the other two components. However, adaptive learning is the most prominent component with the highest (r + c) value of 7.518.

Therefore, in the big data aspect, real-time mining is the most influential component and should be enhanced and promoted first, followed by embedded analytics and adaptive learning, as shown in Fig.2. Real-time mining can discover possible signals of social, environmental, or economical risks from embedded analytics in real-time, and trigger adaptive learning mechanism for safety and security improvement.

4.3.3. The Service Layer

For the service perspective in Table 12, surveillance and customization were the two most causal components, with the highest $(r - c)$ values, 0.601 and 0.205, respectively; both were net causes. Moreover, as shown in the service panel of Figure 2, collaboration had the greatest $(r + c)$ value, 6.125, which implies its prominence in the IoT service aspect.

Hence in the service aspect, surveillance is the most influential component and should be enhanced first, followed by customization and collaboration, as shown in Fig.3. A surveillance component can monitor behavior patterns of individual person or thing, and reduce the cost of service customization or collaboration with the other persons or things.

4.3.4. The Device Layer

According to Table 12, within the device layer, this study found that public facility and business machinery were the two most important component, with the first and second highest (r + c) values, 4.067 and 4.027, respectively. However, personal auxiliary and public facility were the net causal factors with the highest positive (R − D) values, 0.868 and 0.386, respectively. Business machinery was in the net effect group, with a negative (r − c) value of −1.254. As shown in the device panel of Figure 2, personal auxiliary and public facility should be improved first, under the device aspect. These two components are net causes, and influence another component. Moreover, although personal auxiliary is with smaller (r + c) value, improving its sustainability might result in positive influences on the entire smart systems, from a cause-effect viewpoint.

Thus, in the device aspect, personal auxiliary is the most influential component and should be improved and promoted first, followed by public facility and business machinery, as shown in Figure 1. The implication here is that a personal auxiliary or a public facility can be used for safety and health functionality and has direct impacts on social and environmental performance.

5. Conclusions

The aspects and components outlined in this study serve as bridging mechanisms for the evaluation of sustainability of IoT-enabled smart systems. Previous studies did not address the IoT components, whereas this study attempts not only to identify the critical components in the smart systems, but also helps to determine the interrelationships among factors in the IoT-enabled smart systems.

The main contributions of this study are twofold. First, the evaluation of sustainable smart systems is a decision-making problem that is composed of complex dependencies and interactions. In this paper, the underlying layered modular architecture framework was used as a basis to develop a decision framework, to evaluate sustainability in the IoT-enabled smart system. Second, the decision framework and DEMATEL method were combined to analyze and illustrate the complex interactions and interdependencies among aspects and components, and to produce results that allow a visual cause-effect diagram to be constructed, to evaluate the various dependency processes in a smart system. In particular, these complex influencing factors are divided into two groups – causal and effect – and a cause-effect relationship diagram is constructed. Additionally, it is demonstrated that the results could provide guidance to engineers and managers by identifying the key components for decision-making, and finding the best way to improve the existing sustainability in the smart system.

Furthermore, the results of this study are applicable to all frameworks with problems that require segmenting complex factors and determining their importance. In addition, this study suggests an effective approach to continuously improve the overall sustainability in a smart system, in a comprehensive manner.

Moreover, it is demonstrated that the results could provide guidance to managers and engineers by identifying the key criteria for decision-making, and determining the best approach to ensure the sustainability of IoT-enabled smart systems.

Finally, future research could apply other approach, such as the analytic hierarchical process (AHP) or the fuzzy version of the DEMATEL method, to make the comparisons to gain additional insights for finding critical impact factors affecting the sustainability of smart systems.

References

Agarwal, N., & Brem, A. (2015). Strategic business transformation through technology convergence: implications from General Electrics industrial internet initiative. *International Journal of Technology Management, 67*(2/3/4), 196-214.

Atzori, L., Iera, A., & Morabito, G. (2010). The Internet of Things: A survey. *Computer Networks, 54*(15), 2787-2805. doi:10.1016/j.comnet.2010.05.010

Balaji, M. S., & Roy, S. K. (2017). Value co-creation with Internet of things technology in the retail industry. *Journal of Marketing Management, 33*(1/2), 7-31. doi:10.1080/0267257X.2016.1217914

Baucas, M. J., & Spachos, P. (2020). A scalable IoT-fog

framework for urban sound sensing. *Computer Communications, 153*, 302-310.

Benias, N., & Markopoulos, A. P. (2017). *A review on the readiness level and cyber-security challenges in Industry 4.0.* Paper presented at the Design Automation, Computer Engineering, Computer Networks and Social Media Conference (SEEDA-CECNSM), 2017 South Eastern European.

Borgia, E. (2014). The Internet of Things vision: Key features, applications and open issues. *Computer Communications, 54*, 1-31. doi:10.1016/j.comcom.2014.09.008

Braccini, A. M., & Margherita, E. G. (2019). Exploring organizational sustainability of industry 4.0 under the triple bottom line: The case of a manufacturing company. *Sustainability, 11*(1), 36.

Bradley, D., Russell, D., Ferguson, I., Isaacs, J., MacLeod, A., & White, R. (2015). The Internet of Things – The future or the end of mechatronics.

Mechatronics, 27, 57-74. doi:10.1016/j.mechatronics.2015.02.005

Cheng, Y., Tao, F., Xu, L., & Zhao, D. (2018). Advanced manufacturing systems: supply–demand matching of manufacturing resource based on complex networks and Internet of Things. *Enterprise Information Systems, 12*(7), 780-797.

Chiu, M.-C., Chang, C.-H., Chen, Y.-T., Chiou, J.-Y., & Chang, Y.-J. (2016). Redesign for sustainability and assemblability using particle swarm optimization method. *Journal of Industrial & Production Engineering, 33*(2), 103-113. doi:10.1080/21681015.2015.1111264

Day, G. S. (1994). The Capabilities of Market-Driven Organizations. *Journal of Marketing, 58*(4), 37-52. doi:10.2307/1251915

Eskerod, P., Hollensen, S., Morales-Contreras, M. F., & Arteaga-Ortiz, J. (2019). Drivers for Pursuing Sustainability through IoT Technology within High-

End Hotels—An Exploratory Study. *Sustainability (Basel, Switzerland), 11*(19), 5372. doi:10.3390/su11195372

Fontela, E., & Gabus, A. (1976). *The DEMATEL observer, DEMATEL 1976 report*. Geneva, Switzerland: Battelle Geneva Research Center, Geneva.

Gubbi, J., Buyya, R., Marusic, S., & Palaniswami, M. (2013). Internet of Things (IoT): A vision, architectural elements, and future directions. *Future Generation Computer Systems, 29*(7), 1645-1660. doi:10.1016/j.future.2013.01.010

Hammer, J., & Pivo, G. (2017). The triple bottom line and sustainable economic development theory and practice. *Economic Development Quarterly, 31*(1), 25-36.

Huh, S., Cho, S., & Kim, S. (2017). *Managing IoT devices using blockchain platform*. Paper presented at the 2017 19th international conference on advanced communication technology (ICACT).

Jin, J., Gubbi, J., Marusic, S., & Palaniswami, M. (2014). An information framework for creating a smart city through internet of things. *IEEE Internet of Things Journal, 1*(2), 112-121.

Khan, M. A., & Salah, K. (2018). IoT security: Review, blockchain solutions, and open challenges. *Future Generation Computer Systems, 82*, 395-411.

Krotov, V. (2017). The Internet of Things and new business opportunities. *Business Horizons, 60*(6), 831-841. doi:https://doi.org/10.1016/j.bushor.2017.07.009

Lee, I., & Lee, K. (2015). The Internet of Things (IoT): Applications, investments, and challenges for enterprises. *Business Horizons, 58*(4), 431-440. doi:10.1016/j.bushor.2015.03.008

Lin, Y.-T., Yang, Y.-H., Kang, J.-S., & Yu, H.-C. (2011). Using DEMATEL method to explore the core competences and causal effect of the IC design service company: An empirical case study. *Expert Systems with Applications, 38*(5), 6262-6268. doi:10.1016/j.eswa.2010.11.092

Lo, F.-Y., & Campos, N. (2018). Blending Internet-of-Things (IoT) solutions into relationship marketing strategies. *Technological Forecasting and Social Change, 137*, 10-18.

Miorandi, D., Sicari, S., De Pellegrini, F., & Chlamtac, I. (2012). Internet of things: Vision, applications and research challenges. *Ad Hoc Networks, 10*(7), 1497-1516. doi:10.1016/j.adhoc.2012.02.016

Morgan, N. A., Slotegraaf, R. J., & Vorhies, D. W. (2009). Linking marketing capabilities with profit growth. *International Journal of Research in Marketing, 26*(4), 284-293.

Ng, I., Scharf, K., Pogrebna, G., & Maull, R. (2015). Contextual variety, Internet-of-Things and the choice of tailoring over platform: Mass customisation strategy in supply chain management.

International Journal of Production Economics, 159, 76-87. doi:10.1016/j.ijpe.2014.09.007

Novo, O. (2018). Blockchain meets IoT: An architecture for scalable access management in IoT. *IEEE Internet of Things Journal, 5*(2), 1184-1195.

Pal, A., & Kant, K. (2018). IoT-based sensing and communications infrastructure for the fresh food supply chain. *Computer, 51*(2), 76-80.

Porter, M. E., & Heppelmann, J. E. (2015). How smart, connected products are transforming companies. *Harvard Business Review, 93*(10), 96-16. Retrieved from http://search.ebscohost.com/login.aspx?direct=true&db=bth&AN=109338341&lang=zh-tw&site=ehost-live

Reyna, A., Martín, C., Chen, J., Soler, E., & Díaz, M. (2018). On blockchain and its integration with IoT. Challenges and opportunities. *Future Generation Computer Systems, 88*, 173-190.

Si, S.-L., You, X.-Y., Liu, H.-C., & Zhang, P. (2018). DEMATEL technique: A systematic review of the state-of-the-art literature on methodologies and applications. *Mathematical Problems in Engineering, 2018.*

Su, C.-M., Horng, D.-J., Tseng, M.-L., Chiu, A. S., Wu, K.-J., & Chen, H.-P. (2016). Improving sustainable supply chain management using a novel hierarchical grey-DEMATEL approach. *Journal of Cleaner Production, 134*, 469-481.

Tang, M. T., Tzeng, G.-H., & Wang, S.-W. (1999). A hierarchy fuzzy MCDM method for studying electronic marketing strategies in the information service industry. *Journal of International Information Management, 8*(1), 1.

Venters, C. C., Capilla, R., Betz, S., Penzenstadler, B., Crick, T., Crouch, S., . . . Carrillo, C. (2018). Software sustainability: Research and practice from a software architecture viewpoint. *Journal of*

Systems and Software, 138, 174-188.

Weber, R. H. (2010). Internet of Things – New security and privacy challenges. *Computer Law & Security Review, 26*(1), 23-30. doi:10.1016/j.clsr.2009.11.008

Weinberg, B. D., Milne, G. R., Andonova, Y. G., & Hajjat, F. M. (2015). Internet of Things: Convenience vs. privacy and secrecy. *Business Horizons, 58*(6), 615-624. doi:https://doi.org/10.1016/j.bushor.2015.06.005

Weng, W. H. (2020a). *Impacts of Competitive Uncertainty on Supply Chain Competence and Big Data Analytics Utilization: An Information Processing View.* Paper presented at the The International Conference on Electronic Business (ICEB), Hong Kong.

Weng, W. H. (2020b). *Internet of Things Utilization in Marketing for Competitive Advantage: An Organizational Capability Perspective.* Paper presented at the The International Conference on Electronic Business (ICEB), Hong Kong.

Weng, W. H., & Lin, W. T. (2014). *Development assessment and strategy planning in mobile computing industry.* Paper presented at the 2014 IEEE International Conference on Management of Innovation and Technology, Singapore.

Weng, W. H., & Lin, W. T. (2015). A mobile computing technology foresight study with scenario planning approach. *International Journal of Electronic Commerce Studies, 6*(2), 223-232. doi:10.7903/ijecs.1242

Wu, W.-W., Lan, L. W., & Lee, Y.-T. (2011). Exploring decisive factors affecting an organization's SaaS adoption: A case study. *International Journal of Information Management, 31*(6), 556-563. doi:10.1016/j.ijinfomgt.2011.02.007

Yoo, Y., Henfridsson, O., & Lyytinen, K. (2010). The new organizing logic of digital innovation: an agenda for information systems research. *Information systems research, 21*(4), 724-735.

Yu, X., Nguyen, B., & Chen, Y. (2016). Internet of things capability and alliance. *Internet Research, 26*(2), 402-434.

Zhou, W., & Piramuthu, S. (2018). IoT security perspective of a flexible healthcare supply chain. *Information Technology and Management, 19*(3), 141-153. doi:10.1007/s10799-017-0279-7

Chapter 2
Sustainable Systems Development

Abstract

In the era of global environment disasters, coronavirus outbreak, and financial turmoil, developing sustainable information systems is a crucial management task for ensuring the functionality of enterprise information processing and thus sustaining competitiveness. This study develops a set of criteria for sustainable information systems using decision making trial and evaluation laboratory (DEMATEL) method. By referring to the theory of knowledge-based view and sustainability, this study constructed a research framework in which the selection attributes reflect core knowledge elements of a sustainable information system. An empirical study was performed using DEMATEL method with data collected from industry experts. The results conclude a cause and effect relationship of the knowledge factors influencing information system sustainability. The study discovered that the economical aspect is a cause factor of environmental aspect and social aspect for sustainability considerations. Furthermore, commercial IT solution knowledge, eco-design knowledge, and workplace safety and health knowledge are the most influential knowledge components for economic, environmental, and social aspect of information system sustainability respectively.

Keywords: knowledge-based view; sustainability; information system; DEMATEL

1. Introduction

Firms worldwide rely heavily on their information systems for effective operations towards corporate sustainability (Braccini & Margherita, 2019). Information systems are developed with multiple roles in enterprise operations (Tang, Tzeng, & Wang, 1999). Enterprises employ managerial staffs for decision making using services provided by information systems. Sales and customer service staffs rely heavily on information systems for introducing and promoting products and services to corporate users. These various roles form a value network by participating and contributing to the value of enterprises. In an era of rapid product lifecycles with emergent information technologies such as big data analytics (Weng, 2020a; Weng & Lin, 2014b), cloud computing (Wu, Lan, & Lee, 2011), and smart mobile devices (Porter & Heppelmann, 2015; Weng, 2020b; Weng & Lin, 2014a), information systems become even more critical for enterprises.

As the concept of sustainability emerges, the development and use of information systems are required to be aligned with the goal of corporate sustainability. However, determining the factors influencing the sustainability of information systems is complex, and research in this regard is scant so far. The goal of this paper is to fill this gap by proposing a systematic process to analyze critical factors which affect information system sustainability. Furthermore, since the development and maintenance of information systems are highly knowledge intensive, knowledge plays an important role for sustainable information systems. This study utilizes knowledge-based perspective as the theoretical background for extracting the critical factors in the decision process.

The paper begins with a review of the theoretical background about knowledge-based view and sustainability for information systems. Critical factors of sustainable information systems are collected from selected experts in Taiwan. Then it explains the DEMATEL method (Fontela & Gabus, 1976). Following that, the DEMATEL method is applied to analyze the data collected from the experts. Finally, the findings are presented along with managerial implications of the study and suggestions for further research.

2. Materials and Methods
2.1. Theoretical Background
2.1.1. A Knowledge-Based View of Information Systems

The knowledge-based view (KBV) is an outgrowth of resource-based thinking where the concept of resources is extended to include intangible assets and, specifically, knowledge-based resources. Some researchers see KBV as a useful extension of organizational learning to strategy and organization theory, an extension that is capable of informing research and providing new insights into organizational functioning (Eisenhardt & Santos, 2002; Grant, 1996). From the view of an organization, knowledge is the absorbed and assimilated information for organizational operations, and intelligence is the knowledge gathered and organized for decision making (Porter & Millar, 1985).

Information systems help firms deal with uncertainty in business decisions and actions (Weng, 2020a). Nowadays, organizations are facing even greater challenge in decision making than before, as the information to be processed is growing rapidly in volume, velocity and variety (Johnson, Friend, & Lee, 2017). Functions of information systems are cultivated through knowledge acquisition with organizational learning. The knowledge that firms acquire for pursuing and developing business strategy is an important resource for the development of innovative information systems (Porter & Millar, 1985; Smith, McKeen, & Singh, 2007).

The most fundamental knowledge for information system development is IT domain knowledge (Hasselbring, 2000; Shen, Wall, Zaremba, Chen, & Browne, 2004). Participants of the system development lifecycle need to be knowledgeable in information technology to provide decisions on benefits and risks of various IT solutions. However, IT domain knowledge alone cannot support sustainable information system integration. Enterprise information systems are built to facilitate business processes and regulations in the industry sector of the enterprises. There is complex business domain knowledge for each industry sector. Vendors, integrators, and consultants in the system development value network are expected to be more informative than the corporate users in business domains and provide consultancy to incorporate business knowledge in information systems (Shen et al., 2004).

In addition to IT domain knowledge and business domain knowledge, environment domain knowledge and social domain knowledge are becoming a prominent competence for information system development because of the increasing attention of corporate social responsibility (Choi & Hwang, 2015; Tseng, Wu, Ma, Kuo, & Sai, 2019) and corporate citizenship (Carroll, 1998; Di Domenico, Tracey, & Haugh, 2009; Kruggel, Tiberius, & Fabro, 2020). Green IT (Faucheux & Nicolaï, 2011) and green IS (Anthony Jr, 2019) require substantial environmental domain knowledge. For sustainable information system integration, the knowledge spans resource efficient methodologies (Anthony Jr, 2019; Fernández-Robin, Celemín-Pedroche, Santander-Astorga, & Alonso-Almeida, 2019; J.-W. Huang & Li, 2017; Yu, Chavez, Feng, Wong, & Fynes, 2020), environment-friendly technologies (Day & Schoemaker, 2011; Mathews & Reinert, 2014), green supply chain operations (Hervani, Helms, & Sarkis, 2005; Hwang, Huang, & Wu, 2016; Sarkis, Zhu, & Lai, 2011), and application of innovative IT for green (Faucheux &

Nicolaï, 2011; Lokers, Knapen, Janssen, van Randen, & Jansen, 2016).

2.1.2. Sustainability for Information Systems

Sustainability is measured with the triple bottom line (TBL): economical, environmental, and social performances (Braccini & Margherita, 2019). A firm's performances in these three dimensions need to be well balanced. Sustainability has become a critical objective in the entire life cycle of the design, development, and maintenance of corporate products and services (Chiu, Chang, Chen, Chiou, & Chang, 2016). However, the studies in the sustainability perspective are still rare for information systems.

Sustainability is often discussed together with corporate ethics. The two topics are tightly related to each other. While the concepts of ethics and sustainability have gained attention from corporations, the perceptions of firms on these concepts are widely divided (Chun, 2019; Searcy & Buslovich, 2014). Sustainability may imply different things to different organizations. This difference is intensified by the fact that different organizations use sustainability reports differently (Searcy & Buslovich, 2014). Also, views of corporate ethics may differ for different organizations. For example, American enterprises tend to emphasize different ethics measures with European enterprises (Chun, 2019). Previous research also pointed out that there are a large number of recognized drivers for the corporate sustainability concept that may affect corporations. The question of how to manage and balance the diversity of these drivers may cause challenges for corporate leaders. (Lozano, 2015).

Sustainability has become a critical measure in the entire life cycle of the design, development, and maintenance of corporate products and services (Chiu et al., 2016). Some measurement models for sustainability have been proposed for information system development, such as the GreenSoft model (Naumann, Dick, Kern, & Johann, 2011; Venters et al., 2018). However, the studies in the sustainability perspective are still rare for information systems.

Moreover, sustainability is measured with three dimensions: economical, environmental, and social performances (Braccini & Margherita, 2019). A firm's performances in these three dimensions need to be well balanced. Thus in the development and adoption of information systems, factors influencing the performances in these three dimensions need to be considered simultaneously (Venters et al., 2018). These factors often interact and affect each other. Thus, evaluating and comparing the influences of these factors constitute a multiple-criteria decision making task (Si, You, Liu, & Zhang, 2018; Tang et al., 1999; Wu et al., 2011).

2.2. DEMATEL Method

The decision making trial and evaluation laboratory (DEMATEL) method is an MCDM techniques with applications in various areas (Lin, Yang, Kang, & Yu, 2011; Wu et al., 2011). The DEMATEL method not only deliver a means to visualize the causal relationships among criteria through a cause-effect diagram, but also evaluates the intensity to which the factors influence each other (Si et al., 2018). Thus, it is suitable for the purpose of this study.

The regular DEMATEL (Fontela & Gabus, 1976; Si et al., 2018) method contains four main steps: assessing the initial direct relation matrix by experts, normalizing the direct relation matrix, obtaining the total relation matrix, and producing a causal diagram (Si et al., 2018; Wu et al., 2011).

Let vector D and vector R respectively denote the sum of rows and the sum of columns from the total relation matrix obtained. The dimension $(D + R)$, named prominence, shows how much importance the factor has. The dimension (D − R), named relation, divides factors into a cause group and an effect group. A factor is in the cause group if its (D − R) value is positive. A factor is in the effect group if its (D − R) value is negative (Fontela & Gabus, 1976; Wu et al., 2011).

The computing steps of the DEMATEL method can be further described as follows.

The generation of the direct relation matrix

The magnitude of the relationship between factors i and j can be represented by scales according to the following numerical levels: no influence = 0, low influence = 1, medium influence = 2, high influence = 3, and very high influence = 4.

An initial direct relation matrix Z is a n×n matrix obtained by averaging the pair-wise comparisons of experts in terms of impacts and directions between factors, in which zij is expressed as the degree to which the factor i affects the factor j, where $1 \leq i, j \leq n$.

$$Z = [z_{ij}]_{n \times n} \qquad (1)$$

where all principal diagonal elements are equal to zero in Z.

The normalization of the direct relation matrix

The computation of the normalized direct relation matrix $Y = [y_{ij}]$, where $0 \leq y_{ij} \leq 1$, is performed through equations (2) and (3), in which all principal diagonal elements are equal to zero.

$$Y = f \times Z \qquad (2)$$

where

$$f = \frac{1}{max_{1 \leq i \leq n} \sum_{j=1}^{n} z_{ij}} \qquad (3)$$

The computation of the total relation matrix

Once the normalized direct relation matrix Y is obtained, the total relation matrix T can be acquired by using equation (4), in which I denotes the n×n identity matrix and $(I-Y)-1$ is the inversion of the $(I-Y)$ matrix.

$$T = Y \times (I - Y)^{-1} \qquad (4)$$

The exhibition of the causal diagram

The sum of rows and the sum of columns are separately denoted as D and R in equations (5)-(7):

$$T = [t_{ij}]_{n \times n}, \quad i,j = 1, 2, \ldots, n \qquad (5)$$
$$D = \left[\sum_{j=1}^{n} t_{ij}\right]_{n \times 1} \qquad (6)$$
$$R = \left[\sum_{i=1}^{n} t_{ij}\right]_{1 \times n} \qquad (7)$$

In these equations, vector D and vector R are the sum of rows and the sum of columns from the total relation matrix T, respectively.

A cause and effect diagram is also called a causal diagram and is depicted using the values of D and R obtained from equations (6) and (7). A causal diagram is acquired by drawing the points of (D + R, D − R) on the two-dimensional plane, where the horizontal dimension

(D + R) is obtained by adding R to D and the vertical dimension (D − R) is obtained by subtracting R from D.

2.3. The Decision Process

This study conducted literature review and industry expert interviews to collect the possible knowledge components for sustainable information systems. The related area encompasses the triple bottom line (Braccini & Margherita, 2019). Factors proposed by the experts and supported by the literature are listed in Table 1.

Table 1. Knowledge components for information system sustainability.

Aspect	SN	Key Knowledge Component
A1 Economical	K01	Commercial IT solution knowledge
	K02	Business process knowledge
	K03	Software engineering knowledge
	K04	System integration knowledge
A2 Environmental	K05	Green IT knowledge
	K06	Green business model knowledge
	K07	Green software engineering knowledge
	K08	Eco-design knowledge
A3 Social	K09	Corporate citizenship knowledge
	K10	Workplace safety and health knowledge
	K11	Social competitive knowledge
	K12	Social marketing knowledge

The experts then assessed the influence of each factor in pairs by using equation (1) described above. The final results were then computed using equations (2)-(7). The meaning and significance of these factors are elaborated as follows.

2.3.1. Knowledge Components of the Economical Aspect

The economical aspect of information systems mainly reflects how information systems are developed and maintained in efficient and effective ways, so that the systems can fulfill their intended purposes. To meet the economic considerations, knowledge of commercial IT solutions is essential for selecting the available commercial IT products and services that fit the budget and time constraint (Omoumi et al., 2021). Also, since in most cases information systems are digital automation of business processes, competence with business process knowledge is also mandatory (Baiyere, Salmela, & Tapanainen, 2020). Furthermore, knowledge about the methodology and practices of software engineering is required for the entire lifecycle of system development. Finally, knowledge of system integration is indispensable to deal with the integration of various software and hardware components and subsystems.

2.3.2. Knowledge Components of the Environmental Aspect

The environmental aspect of sustainable information systems focuses on enhancing the environmental benefit in the lifecycle of information system development. Green IT knowledge is required for adopting the methodologies of system development that minimize environmental impacts (A. H. Huang, 2009). Green business model knowledge helps the integration of information systems with environmental value creation (Sarkar, Qian, & Peau, 2020). Green software engineering knowledge (Naumann et al., 2011; Venters et al., 2018) and eco-design knowledge (Brambila-Macias & Sakao, 2021; Mendoza, Sharmina, Gallego-Schmid, Heyes, & Azapagic, 2017) provide models and disciplines for environmental-friendly and eco-friendly information systems.

2.3.3. Knowledge Components of the Social Aspect

The knowledge components of the social aspect are crucial to coping with the possible social impacts of information systems. Corporate citizenship knowledge is useful in guiding the development of information systems toward social responsibility (Akbari & McClelland, 2020). In the entire system development lifecycle, workplace safety and health knowledge are required for the safety and health of all stakeholders (Sorensen et al., 2018). Social competitive knowledge (Rajković, Đurić, Zarić, & Glauben, 2021) and social marketing knowledge (Shawky, Kubacki, Dietrich, & Weaven, 2019) provides competitive intelligence and effective marketing campaigns through social activities and media, thus these knowledge components can promote social credence of information systems.

3. Results

Based on the knowledge elements stated above as in Table 1, this research has further employed the DEMATEL method to capture the complex relationships among these factors. As the purpose of the study was to analyze the decision factors and their causal relationships in information system sustainability, a fourth aspect, A4 for information system, was added into the DEMATEL calculation of the relationships among aspects.

The collected pairwise comparison results have been obtained (the comparison mechanism has been described at step 1 of the DEMATEL method), and that the preliminary average direct relation matrix is shown in Tables 2a-2d. Based on the direct relation matrix, these numbers are normalized continuously into the normalized relation matrix (calculated by equations (2) and (3)). The total relation matrix is then obtained by using equation (4).

3.1. The Initial Direct Relation Matrices

The collected pairwise comparison results were obtained (the comparison mechanism has been described at step 1 of the DEMATEL method), and that the preliminary average direct relation matrix is shown in Tables 2a-2d.

Table 2a. Direct relation matrix of the four aspects.

	A1	A2	A3	A4
A1	0.000	2.286	2.571	2.714
A2	2.143	0.000	3.714	2.000
A3	1.857	3.286	0.000	2.000
A4	2.429	1.429	1.429	0.000

Table 2b. Direct relation matrix of economical aspect.

	K01	K02	K03	K04
K01	0.000	1.714	2.857	2.714
K02	1.286	0.000	1.857	1.857
K03	2.857	2.000	0.000	2.857
K04	2.714	1.429	2.714	0.000

Table 2c. Direct relation matrix of environmental aspect.

	K05	K06	K07	K08
K05	0.000	1.571	2.714	1.857
K06	1.571	0.000	2.143	3.000
K07	3.143	1.571	0.000	2.429
K08	3.000	3.143	3.286	0.000

Table 2d. Direct relation matrix of social aspect.

	K09	K10	K11	K12
K09	0.000	3.429	1.857	2.000
K10	3.714	0.000	2.429	3.000
K11	2.143	1.714	0.000	3.143
K12	2.714	2.286	3.571	0.000

3.2. The Normalized Direct Relation Matrices

The direct relation matrices were normalized continuously into the normalized relation matrices by using equations (2) and (3). The results are shown in Tables 3a-3d.

Table 3a. Normalized direct relation matrix of the four aspects.

	A1	A2	A3	A4
A1	0.000	0.291	0.327	0.345
A2	0.273	0.000	0.473	0.255
A3	0.236	0.418	0.000	0.255
A4	0.309	0.182	0.182	0.000

Table 3b. Normalized direct relation matrix of economical aspect.

	K01	K02	K03	K04
K01	0.000	0.222	0.370	0.352
K02	0.167	0.000	0.241	0.241
K03	0.370	0.259	0.000	0.370
K04	0.352	0.185	0.352	0.000

Table 3c. Normalized direct relation matrix of environmental aspect.

	K05	K06	K07	K08
K05	0.000	0.167	0.288	0.197
K06	0.167	0.000	0.227	0.318
K07	0.333	0.167	0.000	0.258
K08	0.318	0.333	0.348	0.000

Table 3d. Normalized direct relation matrix of social aspect.

	K09	K10	K11	K12
K09	0.000	0.375	0.203	0.219
K10	0.406	0.000	0.266	0.328
K11	0.234	0.187	0.000	0.344
K12	0.297	0.250	0.391	0.000

3.3. The Total Relation Matrices

After the normalized relation matrices were obtained, the total relation matrices were then computed by using equation (4). The results are shown in Tables 4a-4d.

Table 4a. Total relation matrix of the four aspects.

	A1	A2	A3	A4
A1	1.788	2.163	2.317	2.103
A2	2.080	2.040	2.505	2.130
A3	1.934	2.195	2.034	1.999
A4	1.592	1.621	1.724	1.401

Table 4b. Total relation matrix of economical aspect.

	K01	K02	K03	K04
K01	1.922	1.662	2.283	2.274
K02	1.540	1.077	1.652	1.654
K03	2.263	1.740	2.087	2.358
K04	2.110	1.582	2.195	1.936

Table 4c. Total relation matrix of environmental aspect.

	K05	K06	K07	K08
K05	0.667	0.690	0.909	0.782
K06	0.879	0.614	0.944	0.930
K07	1.004	0.762	0.775	0.898
K08	1.173	1.023	1.222	0.872

Table 4d. Total relation matrix of social aspect.

	K09	K10	K11	K12
K09	1.551	1.675	1.612	1.662
K10	2.111	1.646	1.907	1.985
K11	1.658	1.486	1.384	1.670
K12	1.933	1.739	1.886	1.642

3.4. The Cause and Effect Relations

After the total relation matrices were obtained by using equation (4), equations (5)-(7) were utilized to compute the cause and effect relations. The results are shown in Table 5.

Table 5. Prominence and relation values.

Factor	D	R	D + R	D - R
A1	8.371	7.393	15.764	0.978
A2	8.755	8.019	16.773	0.736
A3	8.162	8.580	16.742	-0.418
A4	6.337	7.633	13.971	-1.296
K01	8.141	7.835	15.976	0.306
K02	5.922	6.061	11.983	-0.139
K03	8.448	8.216	16.664	0.232
K04	7.822	8.221	16.044	-0.399
K05	3.047	3.724	6.771	-0.676
K06	3.367	3.089	6.455	0.278
K07	3.439	3.850	7.290	-0.411
K08	4.290	3.481	7.771	0.810
K09	6.500	7.253	13.753	-0.754
K10	7.649	6.546	14.195	1.104
K11	6.198	6.789	12.988	-0.591
K12	7.200	6.959	14.159	0.241

3.5. The Causal Diagram

Finally, the causal diagram is produced and displayed in Figure 1 by mapping the dataset of (D + R, D - R) in Tables 5. Based on the data set shown in Table 5, we obtained the bottom left panel of Figure 1, which demonstrates the causal relationships among the four aspects. The other three panels of Figure 1 demonstrate the causal relationships among the components within the aspects of economical (upper left panel), environmental (upper right panel), and social (lower right panel), respectively.

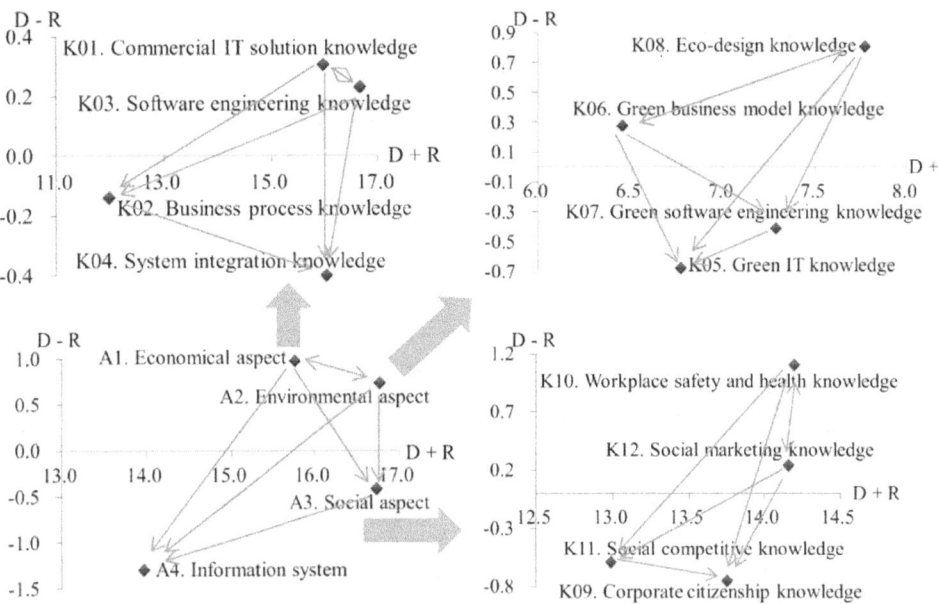

Figure 1. Causal diagram for the sustainability of information systems.

4. Discussion

By examining Figure 1 and Table 5, each factor can be analyzed, and its impact on the overall sustainability discussed. Hence, the critical knowledge components influencing the sustainability of information systems can be determined, as is discussed next.

4.1. The Cause Group and the Effect Group

The results shown in the causal diagrams in Figure 1 have discovered the cause and effect relationships of these core knowledge elements in driving information systems toward sustainability. It is observed that, by looking at these causal diagrams, the factors can be divided into a causal and an effect group. The cause group includes factors with positive (D – R) values, while the effect group includes factors with negative (D – R) values. Since the causal factors have a net impact on the overall framework, their performance can greatly influence the overall goal. Thus, it is generally accepted that the factors in the cause group should be closely monitored. Conversely, the factors in the effect group tend to be easily affected by others, which make them unsuitable as critical impact factors.

Thus, the cause group contains economical aspect (A1), environmental aspect (A2), commercial IT solution knowledge (K01), software engineering knowledge

(K03), eco-design knowledge (K08), green business model knowledge (K06), workplace safety and health knowledge (K10), and social marketing knowledge (K12).

The effect group includes social aspect (A3), information system (A4), business process knowledge (K02), system integration knowledge (K04), green software engineering knowledge (K07), green IT knowledge (K05), social competitive knowledge (K11), and corporate citizenship knowledge (K09).

Therefore, the cause and effect structure in Figure 1 implies that among the knowledge components, K01, K03, K06, K08, K10, and K12 are the main knowledge components in leading information systems to move toward sustainability. Subsequently, knowledge components K02, K04, K05, K07, K09, and K11 are not causal but affected. Thus, they are derived and influenced by the other knowledge components for determining the sustainability of information systems.

4.2. Analysis of the Aspects

As the results exhibited in Table 5 and the bottom left panel of Figure 1 demonstrate, among the four aspects, economical aspect (A1) has the highest (D – R) value, which means that it has a greater impact on the entire framework than it receives from the other aspects. However, environmental aspect (A2) and social aspect (A3) are the two factors with higher (D + R) values, thus they are of high importance in the framework.

The results also reveal that the environmental aspect (A2) is the most important causal factor (with the highest D value) among the three bottom lines, and generates a competitive impact (positive D – R), thus making it the most significant aspect of knowledge to the sustainability of information systems. These guidelines of improvement direction will lead information systems toward a more sustainable level.

These results imply that while knowledge components in the environmental aspect and social aspect are important regarding information system sustainability, they are nevertheless influenced by knowledge components in the economical aspect. Therefore, the utilization of environmental and social domain knowledge in information system development is substantially affected by economical domain knowledge.

4.3. Analysis of Knowledge Components in the Economical Aspect

The results exhibited in Table 5 and the upper left panel of Figure 1 show that, among the knowledge components in the economical aspect, commercial IT solution knowledge (K01) and software engineering knowledge (K03) have positive $(D - R)$ values and thus are causal factors.

The commercial IT solutions for contemporary information systems include many turn key products which already encapsulate business processes (K02) and can facilitate system integration (K04). The system analysis and design phase in software engineering also perform business process analysis. System integration needs to be guided and planned in the subsystem development of software engineering.

Thus, with respect to the economical aspect, commercial IT solution knowledge is the most influential component and should be enhanced first, followed by software engineering knowledge, as shown in Figure 1. These knowledge components expedite successful information system development and reduce the waste of resource and time, thus they help promote sustainability of information systems.

4.4. Analysis of Knowledge Components in the Environmental Aspect

As the results exhibited in Table 5 and the upper right panel of Figure 1 indicate, among the knowledge components in the environmental aspect, eco-design knowledge (K08) and green business model knowledge (K06) have positive (D − R) values and thus are causal factors.

Figure 1 also shows that eco-design knowledge is the most important component with the highest (D + R) value. It has influence on green business model knowledge (K06), green software engineering knowledge (K07) and green IT knowledge (K05). This indicates that eco-design knowledge is the stimulating knowledge components of the other environmental domain knowledge and should be improved and promoted first, followed by green business model knowledge, as shown in Figure 1. Eco-design knowledge is tacitly embedded in many green business practices, and is essential for the environmental-friendliness of system development lifecycle.

4.5. Analysis of Knowledge Components in the Social Aspect

The results exhibited in Table 5 and the lower right panel of Figure 1 show that, among the knowledge components in the social aspect, workplace safety and health knowledge (K10) and social marketing knowledge (K12) have positive (D – R) values and thus are causal factors.

Figure 1 also shows that workplace safety and health knowledge is the most prominent component with the highest (D + R) value. It has influence on social marketing knowledge (K12), social competitive knowledge (K11) and corporate citizenship knowledge (K09). This indicates that workplace safety and health knowledge is the causal knowledge components of the other social domain knowledge and should be improved and promoted first, followed by social marketing knowledge, as shown in Figure 1. Particularly, facing the disastrous COVID-19 outbreaks nowadays, workplace safety and health knowledge is indispensable and inevitable for the social sustainability of system development lifecycle. Its profound impact on the other social domain knowledge and the entire decision framework of sustainable information systems will continue to extend.

5. Conclusions

In conclusion, knowledge factors are essential to the success of engineering and management of information systems. However, past studies have not provided sufficient analysis of the interaction relation among them. Moreover, information system sustainability has emerged in recent years and hence its influencing factors remain unclear. Through the analysis performed, this study has made contributions in the following perspectives: (1) linking knowledge-based view with sustainability; (2) defining the critical knowledge elements for information system sustainability; (3)

investigating the interrelationship of these critical knowledge elements; (4) demonstrating DEMATEL method as an effective multiple criteria decision making tool in supporting the exploration of the cause and effect relationship in a complex decision system; (5) analyzing critical impacts based on the generated casual diagram and providing improvement strategies accordingly.

This study analyzes factors affecting the sustainability of information systems from a knowledge-based perspective. Although knowledge is a critical intangible resource in the development of information systems, other factors are worth further attention. Moreover, the analyzing process in this study can be applied to specialized systems such as medical information systems and FinTech related systems. Further investigations toward these topics are recommended.

References

Akbari, M., & McClelland, R. (2020). Corporate social responsibility and corporate citizenship in sustainable supply chain: a structured literature review. *Benchmarking : an international journal, 27*(6), 1799-1841. doi:10.1108/BIJ-11-2019-0509

Anthony Jr, B. (2019). Green information system integration for environmental performance in organizations: An extension of belief–action–outcome framework and natural resource-based view theory. *Benchmarking : an international journal, 26*(3), 1033-1062. doi:10.1108/BIJ-05-2018-0142

Baiyere, A., Salmela, H., & Tapanainen, T. (2020). Digital transformation and the new logics of business process management. *European Journal of Information Systems, 29*(3), 238-259.

Braccini, A. M., & Margherita, E. G. (2019). Exploring organizational sustainability of industry 4.0 under the triple bottom line: The case of a manufacturing company. *Sustainability, 11*(1), 36.

Brambila-Macias, S. A., & Sakao, T. (2021). Effective ecodesign implementation with the support of a lifecycle engineer. *Journal of Cleaner Production, 279*, 123520. doi:https://doi.org/10.1016/j.jclepro.2020.123520

Carroll, A. B. (1998). The four faces of corporate citizenship. *Business and society review, 100*(1), 1-7.

Chiu, M.-C., Chang, C.-H., Chen, Y.-T., Chiou, J.-Y., & Chang, Y.-J. (2016). Redesign for sustainability and assemblability using particle swarm optimization method. *Journal of Industrial & Production Engineering, 33*(2), 103-113. doi:10.1080/21681015.2015.1111264

Choi, D., & Hwang, T. (2015). The impact of green supply chain management practices on firm performance: the role of collaborative capability.

Operations Management Research, 8(3), 69-83. doi:10.1007/s12063-015-0100-x

Chun, R. (2019). How Virtuous Global Firms Say They Are: A Content Analysis of Ethical Values. *Journal of Business Ethics, 155*(1), 57-73. doi:10.1007/s10551-017-3525-3

Day, G. S., & Schoemaker, P. J. H. (2011). Innovating in Uncertain Markets: 10 Lessons for Green Technologies. *MIT Sloan Management Review, 52*(4), 37-45. Retrieved from <Go to ISI>://WOS:000292572500007

Di Domenico, M., Tracey, P., & Haugh, H. (2009). The dialectic of social exchange: Theorizing corporate—social enterprise collaboration. *Organization studies, 30*(8), 887-907.

Eisenhardt, K. M., & Santos, F. M. (2002). Knowledge-based view: A new theory of strategy. In *Handbook of strategy and management* (Vol. 1, pp. 139-164): Sage Publications.

Faucheux, S., & Nicolaï, I. (2011). IT for green and green IT: A proposed typology of eco-innovation. *Ecological Economics, 70*(11), 2020-2027. doi:10.1016/j.ecolecon.2011.05.019

Fernández-Robin, C., Celemín-Pedroche, M. S., Santander-Astorga, P., & Alonso-Almeida, M. d. M. (2019). Green practices in hospitality: A contingency approach. *Sustainability, 11*(13), 3737.

Fontela, E., & Gabus, A. (1976). *The DEMATEL observer, DEMATEL 1976 report.* Geneva, Switzerland: Battelle Geneva Research Center, Geneva.

Grant, R. M. (1996). Toward a knowledge-based theory of the firm. *Strategic Management Journal, 17*(S2), 109-122.

Hasselbring, W. (2000). Information system integration. *Communications of the ACM, 43*(6), 32-38.

Hervani, A. A., Helms, M. M., & Sarkis, J. (2005). Performance measurement for green supply chain management. *Benchmarking: An international journal, 12*(4), 330-353.

Huang, A. H. (2009). A Model for Environmentally Sustainable Information Systems Development. *The Journal of computer information systems, 49*(4), 114-121. doi:10.1080/08874417.2009.11645346

Huang, J.-W., & Li, Y.-H. (2017). Green Innovation and Performance: The View of Organizational Capability and Social Reciprocity. *Journal of Business Ethics, 145*(2), 309-324. doi:10.1007/s10551-015-2903-y

Hwang, B.-N., Huang, C.-Y., & Wu, C.-H. (2016). A TOE Approach to Establish a Green Supply Chain Adoption Decision Model in the Semiconductor Industry. *Sustainability, 8*(2), 168. doi:10.3390/su8020168

Johnson, J. S., Friend, S. B., & Lee, H. S. (2017). Big Data Facilitation, Utilization, and Monetization: Exploring the 3Vs in a New Product Development

Process. *Journal of Product Innovation Management, 34*(5), 640-658. doi:10.1111/jpim.12397

Kruggel, A., Tiberius, V., & Fabro, M. (2020). Corporate citizenship: Structuring the research field. *Sustainability, 12*(13), 5289.

Lin, Y.-T., Yang, Y.-H., Kang, J.-S., & Yu, H.-C. (2011). Using DEMATEL method to explore the core competences and causal effect of the IC design service company: An empirical case study. *Expert Systems with Applications, 38*(5), 6262-6268. doi:10.1016/j.eswa.2010.11.092

Lokers, R., Knapen, R., Janssen, S., van Randen, Y., & Jansen, J. (2016). Analysis of Big Data technologies for use in agro-environmental science. *Environmental Modelling & Software, 84*, 494-504. doi:https://doi.org/10.1016/j.envsoft.2016.07.017

Lozano, R. (2015). A Holistic Perspective on Corporate Sustainability Drivers. *Corporate Social*

Responsibility & Environmental Management, 22(1), 32-44. doi:10.1002/csr.1325

Mathews, J. A., & Reinert, E. S. (2014). Renewables, manufacturing and green growth: Energy strategies based on capturing increasing returns. *Futures, 61*, 13-22. doi:10.1016/j.futures.2014.04.011

Mendoza, J. M. F., Sharmina, M., Gallego-Schmid, A., Heyes, G., & Azapagic, A. (2017). Integrating backcasting and eco-design for the circular economy: The BECE framework. *Journal of Industrial Ecology, 21*(3), 526-544.

Naumann, S., Dick, M., Kern, E., & Johann, T. (2011). The GREENSOFT Model: A reference model for green and sustainable software and its engineering. *Sustainable Computing: Informatics and Systems, 1*(4), 294-304. doi:https://doi.org/10.1016/j.suscom.2011.06.004

Omoumi, P., Ducarouge, A., Tournier, A., Harvey, H., Kahn, C. E., Louvet-de Verchère, F., . . . Richiardi,

J. (2021). To buy or not to buy—evaluating commercial AI solutions in radiology (the ECLAIR guidelines). *European Radiology, 31*(6), 3786-3796. doi:10.1007/s00330-020-07684-x

Porter, M. E., & Heppelmann, J. E. (2015). How smart, connected products are transforming companies. *Harvard Business Review, 93*(10), 96-16. Retrieved from http://search.ebscohost.com/login.aspx?direct=true&db=bth&AN=109338341&lang=zh-tw&site=ehost-live

Porter, M. E., & Millar, V. E. (1985). How information gives you competitive advantage. *Harvard Business Review, 63*(4), 61-78.

Rajković, B., Đurić, I., Zarić, V., & Glauben, T. (2021). Gaining trust in the digital age: The potential of social media for increasing the competitiveness of small and medium enterprises. *Sustainability, 13*(4), 1884.

Sarkar, A., Qian, L., & Peau, A. K. (2020). Overview of green business practices within the Bangladeshi RMG industry: competitiveness and sustainable development perspective. *Environmental Science and Pollution Research, 27*(18), 22888-22901.

Sarkis, J., Zhu, Q., & Lai, K.-h. (2011). An organizational theoretic review of green supply chain management literature. *International Journal of Production Economics, 130*(1), 1-15. doi:10.1016/j.ijpe.2010.11.010

Searcy, C., & Buslovich, R. (2014). Corporate Perspectives on the Development and Use of Sustainability Reports. *Journal of Business Ethics, 121*(2), 149-169. doi:10.1007/s10551-013-1701-7

Shawky, S., Kubacki, K., Dietrich, T., & Weaven, S. (2019). Using social media to create engagement: a social marketing review. *Journal of social marketing, 9*(2), 204-224. doi:10.1108/JSOCM-05-2018-0046

Shen, H., Wall, B., Zaremba, M., Chen, Y., & Browne, J.

(2004). Integration of business modelling methods for enterprise information system analysis and user requirements gathering. *Computers in Industry, 54*(3), 307-323.

Si, S.-L., You, X.-Y., Liu, H.-C., & Zhang, P. (2018). DEMATEL technique: A systematic review of the state-of-the-art literature on methodologies and applications. *Mathematical Problems in Engineering, 2018*.

Smith, H. A., McKeen, J. D., & Singh, S. (2007). Developing information technology strategy for business value. *Journal of Information Technology Management, 18*(1), 49-58.

Sorensen, G., Sparer, E., Williams, J. A. R., Gundersen, D., Boden, L. I., Dennerlein, J. T., . . . Wagner, G. R. (2018). Measuring Best Practices for Workplace Safety, Health, and Well-Being: The Workplace Integrated Safety and Health Assessment. *Journal of occupational and environmental medicine, 60*(5),

430-439. doi:10.1097/JOM.0000000000001286

Tang, M. T., Tzeng, G.-H., & Wang, S.-W. (1999). A hierarchy fuzzy MCDM method for studying electronic marketing strategies in the information service industry. *Journal of International Information Management, 8*(1), 1.

Tseng, M.-L., Wu, K.-J., Ma, L., Kuo, T. C., & Sai, F. (2019). A hierarchical framework for assessing corporate sustainability performance using a hybrid fuzzy synthetic method-DEMATEL. *Technological Forecasting and Social Change, 144*, 524-533.

Venters, C. C., Capilla, R., Betz, S., Penzenstadler, B., Crick, T., Crouch, S., . . . Carrillo, C. (2018). Software sustainability: Research and practice from a software architecture viewpoint. *Journal of Systems and Software, 138*, 174-188.

Weng, W. H. (2020a). *Impacts of Competitive Uncertainty on Supply Chain Competence and Big Data Analytics Utilization: An Information*

Processing View. Paper presented at the The International Conference on Electronic Business (ICEB), Hong Kong.

Weng, W. H. (2020b). *Internet of Things Utilization in Marketing for Competitive Advantage: An Organizational Capability Perspective.* Paper presented at the The International Conference on Electronic Business (ICEB), Hong Kong.

Weng, W. H., & Lin, W. T. (2014a). *Development assessment and strategy planning in mobile computing industry.* Paper presented at the 2014 IEEE International Conference on Management of Innovation and Technology, Singapore.

Weng, W. H., & Lin, W. T. (2014b). Development trends and strategy planning in big data industry. *Contemporary Management Research, 10*(3).

Wu, W.-W., Lan, L. W., & Lee, Y.-T. (2011). Exploring decisive factors affecting an organization's SaaS adoption: A case study. *International Journal of*

Information Management, 31(6), 556-563. doi:10.1016/j.ijinfomgt.2011.02.007

Yu, W., Chavez, R., Feng, M., Wong, C. Y., & Fynes, B. (2020). Green human resource management and environmental cooperation: An ability-motivation-opportunity and contingency perspective. *International Journal of Production Economics, 219*, 224-235.

Chapter 3
Sustainable Systems Education and Learning

Abstract

During the breakout of coronavirus disease (COVID-19), smart technologies were perceived to provide convenience and assistance for people, enterprises and government units. Although there are literature maintained that smart technology can facilitate pandemic strategy and response in ways that are difficult to achieve manually, some other literature indicated that smart technologies were not desirable alternatives to people during this pandemic. MIS education is a career preparation for IT professionals who use smart technology in organizations. IT professionals with MIS education background may have important roles when facing COVID-19. Moreover, many MIS students will become IT professionals and join the workforce for combatting the pandemic using smart technologies with their background of MIS education. This study intends to construct theories which depict the relevance among MIS education, IT professionals, and smart technologies in the confrontation of the COVID-19 pandemic by in-depth interviews with MIS students. The results could provide reflective insights for MIS education providers, human resource units, IT firms, and organizations confronting COVID-19 outbreaks.

Keywords: management information system, education, learning, IT professional, smart technology, COVID-19, metaphor

1. Introduction

Since the beginning of 2020, the world has been confronting the epidemic of coronavirus disease (COVID-19). To prevent the contagion, many countries have restricted transportation, grounded airlines, closed public facilities, blocked traffics, sealed cities, and quarantine residents, making the provision of goods and services extremely difficult (Whitelaw, Mamas, Topol, & Van Spall, 2020). During this abnormal period, electronic governments and businesses taking the advantage of digital technologies (DT) provide emergency reliefs to the people and organizations in need at home or worldwide under this disastrous situation (Tuli, Tuli, Tuli, & Gill, 2020).

However, the perceptions of using smart technologies to assist the countering of the pandemic are divided. There are literature maintained that digital technology can facilitate pandemic strategy and response in ways that are difficult to achieve manually (Whitelaw et al., 2020). Some other literature indicated that technologies such as smartphones, tablets, and PC were not desirable alternatives to regular voice-based phones during this pandemic (Kjerkol, Linset, & Westeren, 2021). These opposite views on the effectiveness of using smart technologies for coping with the COVID-19 pandemic require further study for deeper insight of pandemic confrontation.

Moreover, IT professionals are key actors of the utilization of smart technologies. They are people with IT skills to help the confrontation of contingencies for governments, enterprises, and other organizations. Therefore, IT professionals could be an important linkage resource between digital technologies and the COVID-19 confrontation. Furthermore, many IT professionals have their education background in management information systems (MIS). Their professional careers start with the knowledge obtained from MIS education. Thus the role of MIS education may also be relevant in the connection between digital technologies and the confrontation with COVID-19. However, despite these possible connections, so far the research on the relations of COVID-19 confrontation, IT professional, and MIS education are very scant. Therefore, the objective of this research is to investigate and clarify the possible linkages.

The paper begins with a review of the relevant literature about the relationships among COVID-19 pandemic, smart technologies, IT professionals, and MIS education. Then it explains the research setting for this study. Following that, the process of data collection and the results of data analysis are elaborated. Finally, discussion with implications and conclusions with suggestions are provided.

2. Research Background
2.1 Smart Technology and COVID-19 Outbreaks

The year of 2020 was a difficult time for the whole world. The outbreak and wide-spread of COVID-19 pandemic changed the lives of many people. During this hard time, governments and enterprises worldwide have utilized various smart technologies to avert further deterioration of the situation (Gong et al., 2020; Weng, 2021c; Whitelaw et al., 2020).

The contemporary smart technology is considered as "the next big thing" (Borgia, 2014; Marinova, de Ruyter, Huang, Meuter, & Challagalla, 2017; Porter & Heppelmann, 2015; Weng, 2021a) by many countries and organizations. Several researchers have elaborated the technological features of the smart technologies (Agarwal & Brem, 2015; Atzori, Iera, & Morabito, 2010; Borgia, 2014; Bradley et al., 2015; Gubbi, Buyya, Marusic, & Palaniswami, 2013; Krotov, 2017; Miorandi, Sicari, De Pellegrini, & Chlamtac, 2012; Porter &

Heppelmann, 2015; Weng & Lin, 2014a, 2014b; Yoo, Henfridsson, & Lyytinen, 2010). In Table 1 these features are classified and summarized using the layered modular architecture (Weng, 2021b; Yoo et al., 2010).

Table 1   Layered modular architecture of smart technologies

Layer	Module	Feature	Reference
Content	Real-time analytics	Sensor monitored and detected information are invisibly embedded in the environment around users, results in the generation of big data in real-time which are distributed, stored, processed, presented and interpreted in a seamless, efficient, and	(Gubbi et al., 2013; Krotov, 2017)

Layer	Module	Feature	Reference
		easily understandable form.	
	Cyber-physical convergence	The convergence of computer network, telecom network and the IoT triggers further convergence of cyber space and physical space, and results in various smart spaces, such as smart home, smart office, smart factory, smart laboratory, smart store, smart marketplace, smart hospital, smart museum and smart city.	(Agarwal & Brem, 2015; Bradley et al., 2015; Gubbi et al., 2013; Miorandi et al., 2012)

Layer	Module	Feature	Reference
Service	Cloud support	Cloud services are deployed to assist the processing and storage of big data analytics, and provide users ubiquitous access of supporting services initiated by devices around the smart environment.	(Atzori et al., 2010; Bradley et al., 2015; Gubbi et al., 2013)
	Intelligent interface	Visualization, touching and voice are critical for smart applications as this allows the awareness and interaction of users with the environment. 3D viewing and printing	(Bradley et al., 2015; Gubbi et al., 2013)

Layer	Module	Feature	Reference
		technologies, personal mobile assistants, wearable devices, and augmented-reality devices provide novel interface for users to interact with the smart environment.	
Network	Pervasive connectivity	Smart mobile devices and the IoT contains multiple layers of communication networking infrastructure to provide the pervasive communications between people and people, people and	(Atzori et al., 2010; Gubbi et al., 2013; Yoo et al., 2010)

Layer	Module	Feature	Reference
		things, and things and things, to form a smart environment.	
	Seamless streaming	Wireless broadband technologies enable robust streaming of digital content data through broadband wireless networks for multimedia applications and services on demand.	(Borgia, 2014; Gubbi et al., 2013; Krotov, 2017)
Device	Ubiquitous sensing	This is the mechanism that the "things" or devices in the IoT perceive the surrounding physical	(Borgia, 2014; Bradley et al., 2015;

Layer	Module	Feature	Reference
		environment, detect and record the changes in the environment, and respond to the changes. Ubiquitous sensing is enabled by wireless sensor network (WSN) technologies.	Gubbi et al., 2013)
	Embedded computing	Smart mobile devices contain embedded hardware and software to work intelligently within the environment. The embedded hardware includes processor chips, data storage units and power units. The embedded	(Gubbi et al., 2013; Krotov, 2017)

Layer	Module	Feature	Reference
		software includes embedded operating systems, mobile apps and middleware. In particular, the devices can be modularly embedded further in other devices.	
	Interconnected smart products	The smart technologies enable evolution of various products such as smart home appliances, robots, drones, unmanned cars, automated factory machines and business equipment, and many	(Krotov, 2017; Miorandi et al., 2012; Porter & Heppelmann, 2015)

Layer	Module	Feature	Reference
		other innovative devices.	

The critical capabilities of smart technologies include the empowerment of highly personalized, customized, and adaptable products and services (Porter & Heppelmann, 2015; Weng, 2022), and the dynamic decision support through situational sensing, monitoring, and learning (Marinova et al., 2017).

With these technological features, smart technologies have been applied in various confrontation scenarios of COVID-19. Table 2 provides examples of applications using smart technologies for confronting COVID-19 epidemic.

Table 2 Examples of IT applications for COVID-19 confrontation

	Government	Business	Individual
Surveillance	Public health status and medical data detection	Employee locations and health status tracing	Personal health information; Footprint timeline tracing
Collaboration	Logistics and distribution of healthcare materials	Remote co-working and employee collaboration; Supply chain flexibility	Social media and instant messaging
Mobilization	Remote public services and distance education	Online marketing and selling; Mobile commerce	Mobile shopping and entertainment on demand

2.2 MIS Education and IT Professionals

Each year, many students graduated from university MIS (or similar) education programs join the workforce of IT professionals, and play a pivotal role in the utilization of digital technologies to serve in various sectors of organizations. Figure 1 exhibits an example of a smart technology curriculum in MIS education program.

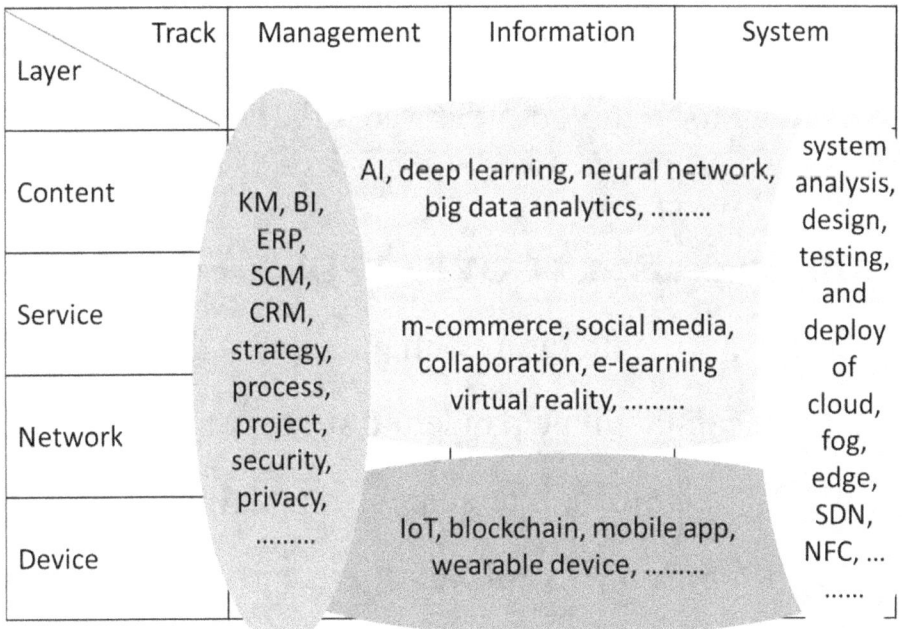

Figure 1 A smart technology curriculum in MIS education program

Figure 1 shows that a core MIS curriculum is designed to invoke the attention and relevance of MIS students to the development and application of smart technologies. With this education background in MIS discipline, they are expected to be confident and perform their duties with satisfying results.

However, the real world is always full of various challenges. Starting from the year of 2020, MIS graduates are facing one more challenge that is not seen in human history: the outbreak of COVID-19.

2.3 MIS Students and COVID-19 Outbreaks

There are literature maintained that digital technology can facilitate pandemic strategy and response in ways that are difficult to achieve manually (Whitelaw et al., 2020). Since MIS education is a career preparation for IT professionals who use digital technology in organizations, MIS education and IT professionals should become critical when facing COVID-19 (Dwivedi et al., 2020).

However, some other literature argued that technologies such as smartphones, tablets, and PC were not desirable alternatives to regular voice-based phones during this pandemic situation (Kjerkol et al., 2021). This counter proposition weakened the role of digital technologies facing COVID-19, thus it may also depreciate the impacts of MIS education and IT professionals on coping with the pandemic (Pflügler, Wiesche, Becker, & Krcmar, 2018).

Therefore, opposite views exist on the connections among MIS education, IT professionals, smart technologies, and COVID-19 confrontation. This contradiction triggers the question that, many MIS students will become IT professionals and join the workforce for combatting the pandemic using digital technologies with their background of MIS education, how do they perceive this issue?

Moreover, COVID-19 outbreak triggered many schools worldwide to enforce a policy of distance education. The Taiwanese students also experienced long hours of learning by remote technology for the first time. This policy also caused many Taiwanese students studying abroad to come back to Taiwan temporarily. Most of them chose to come back to their family and friends to avoid facing the pandemic alone. This experience of disruption in life may have a long term impact on their perceptions of learning and future career.

Therefore, this study aims to answer the following research question: How do MIS students (i.e., the future IT professionals) perceive the meanings and connections about their MIS education, IT professionals, and COVID-19 confrontation?

3. Research Method

3.1 Research Setting and Data Collection

This study intends to construct theoretical framework which depict the relevance among MIS education, IT professionals, and smart technologies in the confrontation of the COVID-19 pandemic. A grounded theory approach is chosen, because of its specific objective of building theory from qualitative data and interpretative analysis (Corbin & Strauss, 1990).

Data for this study were collected through formal interview, participatory observation, archived data, and informal conversation. Data collection activities were started from the middle of April 2021 and took about thirty days to complete. Table 3 exhibits data collection methods.

Table 3   Data Collection

Data source	Data collection process
Formal interviews	• Six formal interviews, each took about eighty minutes • Seventeen follow up video conferences for data clarification • Interviewees include MIS students and recent graduates • We have ruled out the students from our affiliated school
Participatory observation	• Totally seven occasions with average time length of sixty minutes. Include: • two online course meetings • one online homework discussion with classmates • two distance conferences with work colleagues • two occasions of working from home
Archived data	• MIS education program descriptions on the university websites • Recruiting advertisements for IT professionals

Data source	Data collection process
	• Attending two public corporate conferences held by IT companies • Discussion of life and social experience on social media • News and commentaries about COVID-19 outbreaks and social phenomena
Informal dialog	• Five conversations with two MIS professors, one of which has been a department chair • Three conversations with a corporate CIO and an MIS team • Four conversations with a senior VP of a recruitment website

3.3 Recruiting Procedure

This study used a purposive sampling with a snowballing method to recruit participants. In the sampling we have ruled out students of our affiliated school. Data collection by interviews was conducted in April of 2021. Totally six interviewees with diverse background from different universities in Taiwan and USA participated in this study. At the time of the interviews, some of them were senior MIS students, some of them were master level MIS students, and the others were recent graduates from MIS programs and worked for less than two years. Samples are as shown in Table 4. They were interviewed separately. Each interview lasted about eighty minutes.

Table 4 Sample description

Case name	Status at the time of this study	Affiliated school location
Student Chen	<ul><li>Senior undergraduate MIS student</li><li>Studied accounting before transferred to MIS</li><li>Part-time work in pharmacy sector for one year</li></ul>	Northern Taiwan
Student Fang	<ul><li>Senior undergraduate MIS student</li><li>Assisting a project about cloud security and social media privacy</li><li>Summer practicum at a medical equipment manufacturer</li><li>Summer practicum at an online retailer</li></ul>	California, USA
Student Guo	<ul><li>First year master level MIS graduate student</li><li>Two years of working experience in finance sector</li></ul>	Northern Taiwan

Case name	Status at the time of this study	Affiliated school location
	• Part-time working experience at a gym • Self-study of herbal medicine	
Student Lin	• Second year master level MIS graduate student • Working on a thesis about comparing agile development model and waterfall model • One year of working experience in media sector • Part-time volunteer service in healthcare sector	Texas, USA
Student Wu	• Graduated from undergraduate MIS program • Working for two years in the MIS unit of manufacturing sector	Northern Taiwan

Case name	Status at the time of this study	Affiliated school location
	• Travelled to China and Korea several times for work assignment during COVID-19 outbreak	
Student Yeh	• Graduated from master MIS program • Master project of using neural network and data mining to analyze supply chain data • Working for one year in the MIS unit of retail sector • Six months of civil service in a hospital of an outer island of Taiwan	California, USA

3.4 Interview Process

Semi-structured interviews are conducted with the sampled MIS students. Data were recorded through a semi-structured guideline as a starting point, followed by open-ended and unstructured interviews. The semi-structured interview guideline is listed in Table 5. The interviewees are invited to freely express their thoughts about their MIS education, IT professional, and the current COVID-19 situations.

Table 5   Semi-structured interview guideline

Sequence	Topics
1. Opening	
1	Introduction
2. MIS education	
2.1	Reasons of studying MIS
2.2	General perception about MIS education
2.3	Additional thoughts
3. IT professional	
3.1	Interest of becoming an IT professional
3.2	General perception about IT professional
3.3	Additional thoughts
4. COVID-19	
4.1	General perception about COVID-19
4.2	Impacts of COVID-19 to MIS education
4.3	Impacts of COVID-19 to IT professional
4.4	Additional thoughts
5. Ending	
5.1	Acknowledgement and other suggestions

3.5 Data Analysis

The data of this study were analyzed after data collection stage. The interview files were transcribed from notes to text to form the significant statements as the data for analysis in this study. Data clarification was made by contacting the interviewees when there were ambiguous or missing contexts. After reading of the transcribed text, the researcher extracted the meanings of perceptions and experiences of the interviewed students. Iterative meanings were collected, analyzed, coded, and organized into themes.

4. Results

Data from the individual interviews were analyzed and classified into three themes: MIS education as an adaptable incubator, IT professional as an agile integrator, and COVID-19 epidemic as an anguishing intruder.

4.1 MIS Education as an Adaptable Incubator

Excerpts of the interview results of MIS students' perceptions about MIS education were analyzed as shown in Table 6. Three attributes were identified for students' perceptions about MIS education: adaptable content, continuous learning, and intellectual preparation.

Table 6   MIS students' perception of MIS education

Interview excerpt	Coding	Theme
MIS education to me is a fundamental learning of IT and its application. The knowledge is updated very quickly so we have to keep learning by ourselves anytime and anywhere we can.	Intellectual preparation Continuous learning	An adaptable incubator
I think of my MIS education as a training to become a knowledgeable person of information technology and management who is adaptable to new trends.	Intellectual preparation Adaptable content	

Interview excerpt	Coding	Theme
Maybe it is because of the fast changing pace of this discipline. I feel it is like a life-long learning task. We have to continue learning by ourselves even after graduation. The goal is to prepare ourselves for challenging IT tasks. Learning in the clouds is quite popular now. You can find many free courses and training programs in YouTube and other websites. It is your own responsibility to keep learning.	Adaptable content Continuous learning Intellectual preparation	
After the COVID-19 outbreak, most of the times we use distance learning and take courses online. At first I was not used to study this way, but now I get used to it and think it's quite convenient.	Continuous learning	

Interview excerpt	Coding	Theme
I can use my mobile phone to participate courses. Thanks to smart technologies.		
The school teaches you the foundation knowledge. It is like open the door for you. Then you have to go further by yourself. Because new AI and deep learning knowledge are coming up so fast, we need to visit our library and websites very often and keep learning whenever we have time.	Continuous learning Adaptable content	
Fortunately, we have a pretty good digital library in our school. I think it saves me much of the time to find the innovative status of IT related topics. For example, our professors would ask us to log into the school library and search for the recent development of IoT and blockchain.	Adaptable content	

This theme refers to students' experiences and viewpoints about the content and value of their MIS education.

4.2 IT Professional as an Agile Integrator

Excerpts of the interview results of MIS students' perceptions about IT professional were analyzed as shown in Table 7. Attributes identified in this topic include: digital infrastructure, agile servicing, and technology integration.

Table 7　MIS students' perception of IT professional

Interview excerpt	Coding	Theme
IT and IT professionals are seldom regarded as a leading role. It is the infrastructure. It is much like a supportive role. However, it is a	Digital infrastructure Technology integration	An agile integrator

Interview excerpt	Coding	Theme
necessary supportive role for all the other services.		
Manufacturing, finance, retail, healthcare, and even government all require the infrastructure provided by IT. I think of IT professionals as enabling integrators of information systems. Without them, IT is just a piece of hardware.	Digital infrastructure Technology integration	
My understanding about IT professionals is that they often work under very tight schedules because all the others would base on them to function. IT is like an infrastructure to everything.	Digital infrastructure Agile servicing	
It seems to me that they (IT professionals) don't need to have a deep	Technology integration	

Interview excerpt	Coding	Theme
knowledge on every kind of technology, but they need to know how to quickly put things together to work. Smart technologies are advancing very fast, they have to keep up with the technologies and practice them.	Agile servicing	
In this profession we need to deliver innovative services efficiently under time constraint and changing requirements. The user preferences and demands are constantly changing, so we usually work with learning-by-doing to quickly respond to the changing world. So for the COVID-19 situations, we need to work around the needs of our clients, because their situations have	Agile servicing	

Interview excerpt	Coding	Theme
also changed suddenly. We need to think and act ahead of our clients.		
During the COVID-19 pandemic our professors invited some graduates now in healthcare industry to our class and shared how they help mitigating the situation with the integration of smart technologies.	Technology integration	

This theme refers to students' understanding of IT professional from classroom knowledge and previous experiences to the practicum or part-time works by the observation and practice in the workplace settings.

4.3 COVID-19 epidemic as an Anguishing Intruder

Excerpts of the interview results of MIS students' perceptions about COVID-19 epidemic were analyzed as shown in Table 8. The identified attributes in this topic were: lifestyle disruption, pervasive anxiety, and public uncertainty.

Table 8   MIS students' perception of COVID-19 epidemic

Interview excerpt	Coding	Theme
People were wondering how long it (COVID-19) will last, how much food supply is left, and where to get a mask. My parents run a small retail store in the south (of Taiwan). During the pandemic they really worried about the supply of merchandise and the stop of customers.	Public uncertainty Pervasive anxiety	An anguishing intruder
Most of us have to stay home or stay at the dorm. Most of our courses changed to distance learning. We were not allowed to have indoor meetings and activities.	Lifestyle disruption	

Interview excerpt	Coding	Theme
The virus can continue to evolve and mutate. They seem to be unstoppable. So far no really cure is available. We were advised to avoid physical contacts with our family members, classmates, and friends. This is really annoying.	Pervasive anxiety Lifestyle disruption	
There are lots of fake news and false messages of the pandemic situations around. This is often amplified by social media. I think social media need to be used more carefully in time like this. So I think COVID-19 breakout is not just the spread of physical viruses, but also the spread of cyber viruses.	Public uncertainty Pervasive anxiety	
COVID-19 breakout makes me pause my usual activities and think about life,	Lifestyle disruption	

Interview excerpt	Coding	Theme
our environment, and our community. I wonder if there is something I can do to help. You have to respect human lives. You have to respect the environment. You have to respect the ecology. These are what COVID-19 taught us.	Pervasive anxiety	
During this period, we rely on various information systems and services to cope with the situation. Online shopping, distance learning, remote conferencing, and work at home become common for almost everyone. This scenario makes me feel like living in a world of virtual reality.	Lifestyle disruption	

This theme refers to students' cognition and experiences about the COVID-19 outbreaks. They narrated their encountering of the disastrous pandemic and the disruption and change of their lives.

4.4 Summary of Findings

Table 9 exhibits a summary of the findings. In our coding process, metaphors were adopted as a media of scientific communications. Recent research in cognitive science has demonstrated that metaphors can shape the way people think and initiate scientific research ideas through novel comparisons between natural phenomena and everyday experiences (Taylor & Dewsbury, 2018; Thibodeau, Hendricks, & Boroditsky, 2017). Metaphors are also commonly adopted in MIS studies. For example, "cloud" computing, "waterfall" model, and data "warehouse" are all metaphors for understanding abstract concepts of information technologies.

Table 9 Summary of MIS students' perceptions

Subject	Perception	Components
MIS education	As an adaptable incubator	• Adaptable content • Continuous learning • Intellectual preparation
IT Professional	As an agile integrator	• Agile servicing • Digital infrastructure • Technology integration
COVID-19 epidemic	As an anguishing intruder	• Lifestyle disruption • Pervasive anxiety • Public uncertainty

5. Discussion

The results can be further discussed toward five focal points: meanings of the metaphors, linkage of the perceptions, remedy of the pandemic impacts, the role of smart technologies, and the possible transitions. These focal points are illustrated as follows.

5.1 Understanding the metaphors

As displayed in Figure 2, metaphors are widely used in MIS study and IT profession to convey abstract concepts by familiar things in life. In our analysis of data, the students' perceptions of MIS education, IT professional, and COVID-19 outbreak were also expressed with metaphors such as "an adaptable incubator", "an agile integrator", and "an anguishing intruder". We presented these metaphors to various MIS students, IT professionals, and scholars (listed as informal dialog in Table 3) and obtained positive responses. They also suggested that in many scenarios of communicating with IT professionals, using metaphors are more profound and inspiring. The three metaphors we adopted, incubator, integrator, and intruder, also fit the IT culture and lingo.

```
        ┌─────────────┐                                                    ┌─────────────┐
        │    MIS      │                                                    │     IT      │
        │ Education as│        Metaphors in MIS studies                    │ Professional│
        │ an adaptable│      "cloud" computing, "waterfall" model,         │  as an agile│
        │  incubator  │       data "mining", data "warehouse",             │  integrator │
        └─────────────┘        "neural" network, supply "chain",           └─────────────┘
• Continuous learning          cyber "virus", program "bugs"'         • Digital infrastructure
• Adaptable content             "firewall", "gateway", ........       • Agile servicing
• Intellectual preparation                                            • Technology integration


                                  • Public uncertainty
                                  • Pervasive anxiety
                                  • Lifestyle disruption
                              ┌─────────────┐
                              │  Covid-19   │
                              │ Pandemic as an│
                              │  anguishing │
                              │   intruder  │
                              └─────────────┘
```

Figure 2   Understanding the metaphors

5.2 Linking the Perceptions

Figure 3 shows a conceptual framework linking the students' perceptions of MIS education, IT professional, and COVID-19 outbreak. These linkages were constructed in the coding process by relating the attributes of the perceptions in Tables 6-8. For example,

MIS education is an incubator for cultivating digital intellectual of IT professionals, while IT professionals provide experiences of the work on digital infrastructure. Also, the COVID-19 pandemic is expected to extend the adaptable content of MIS education and stimulate effective practices of IT professionals.

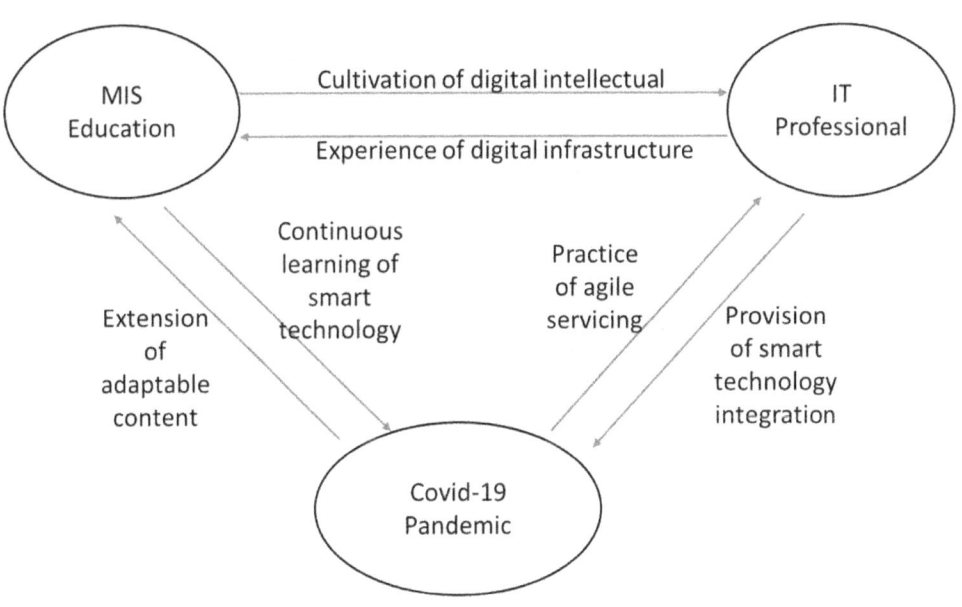

Figure 3 Linking the perceptions

5.3 Remedying the Intruder

Figure 4 displays a framework which elaborates the challenges of the COVID-19 outbreak on the connections between MIS education and IT Professional and the stimulation of topics for MIS learning and IT practices.

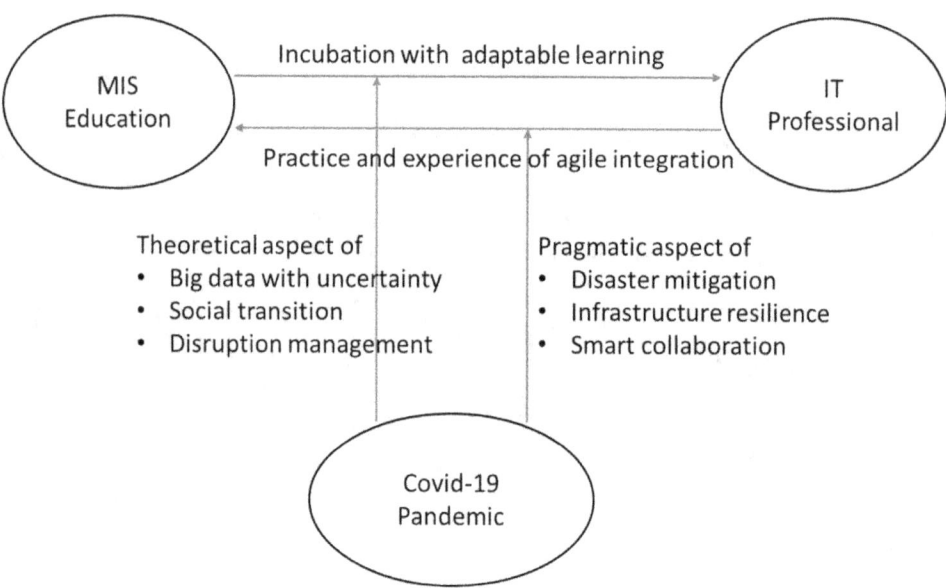

Figure 4　Remedying the intruder

COVID-19 outbreaks have caused lifestyle disruption, pervasive anxiety, and public uncertainty. For

MIS education, these dimensions could activate the study such as big data with uncertainty, social transition, and disruption management. For IT professionals, these dimensions should intensify the practices of infrastructure resilience, disaster mitigation, and smart collaboration. Since the pandemic will not vanish soon, these research and practices will also continue.

Furthermore, the experience of facing COVID-19 is highly personalized and diversified. Everyone may be dealing with different problems and coping with different situations. The decision making is required to adjust dynamically with the fast changing environment. Therefore, making individual life transition facing COVID-19 becomes a challenging problem.

5.4 Exploiting Smart Technologies

In our analysis of the data, we found the role of smart technology quite subtle. It was a hidden role, since we did not specifically asked the interviewees about the perception of smart technology (see Table 5). However, it became clear in the coding process that smart technology is actually a leading role. Its role is inevitable and indispensable. This is further evidenced by our participatory observation (see Table 3).

For example, how could the students achieve their continuous learning and intellectual preparation during the disruptive time of COVID-19 outbreaks? They need to do that using their smart mobile devices through the established digital infrastructure and technology integration. Their learning and adapting are empowered, for example, by smart mobile devices, cloud supported learning, streaming of contents, and cyber-physical convergence for virtual classroom (see Table 1).

Also, how could the IT professionals perform their agile servicing and technology integration practices under COVID-19 disasters? They can only do that efficiently with remote and mobile collaboration of work through smart technologies they had learned since their

MIS education and continuous learning. Their practice and service are empowered, for example, by real-time big data analytics for requirement changes, pervasive connectivity for work collaboration, intelligent interface for prototype demonstration, and embedded computing for product automation (see Table 1).

Moreover, how could we, as members of our society, sustain lifestyle disruption, pervasive anxiety, and public uncertainty caused by COVID-19 pandemic? Various archival data (such as those listed in Table 3) indicated that many people sustained with the help of the mobile app services (see Table 2) from the governments, healthcare providers, social media, online retailers, and volunteer organizations using the digital infrastructure and integrated applications developed by IT professionals.

Figure 5 depicts the empowering of smart technologies for MIS education, IT professionals, and sustainable societies facing COVID-19 outbreaks.

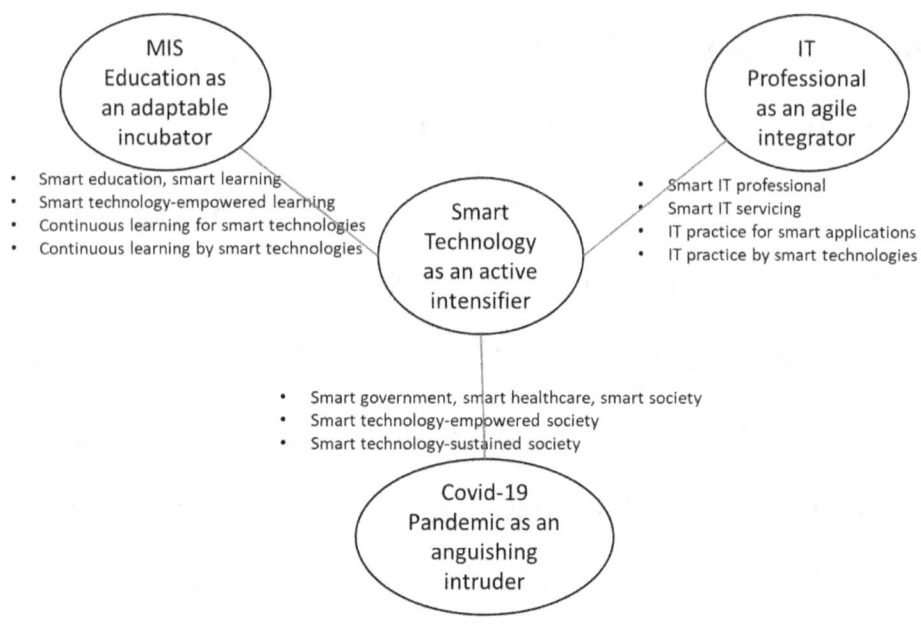

Figure 5   Exploiting smart technologies

5.5 Facilitating the Transition

The examples of MIS students and IT professionals demonstrate the mechanism of smart technology-empowered transition facing COVID-19 outbreaks. They utilized smart technologies to facilitate the transition of their lives during the difficult time of COVID-19 pandemic. Specifically, while the MIS students are learning for smart technologies in their MIS education, they are also using smart technologies to facilitate their learning. Likewise, while the IT professionals are working on the development and integration of smart technologies, they are also using smart technologies to facilitate their work.

After the analyzed results of students' perceptions of MIS education, IT professional, and COVID-19 outbreak were obtained, this study presented the preliminary results to two MIS professors and a corporate MIS team for further discussion (listed as informal dialog in Table 3). They offered their views and suggested applicable transition paths for students from academic and practitioner perspectives respectively. The transition is consistent with the motivation model of learning (Keller, 2016).

The motivation model of learning contains a synthesis of motivational and volitional concepts and theories that provide a foundation for a motivational design process that has been validated in many contexts (Chang, Hu, Chiang, & Lugmayr, 2020; Keller, 2016). In this study we broaden the motivation model from education to include practice and experience. Figure 6 shows a road map of motivating transitions linking MIS student with COVID-19 confrontation.

	Transition of practice and experience			
	Transition	Motivation	Exercise	Action facing COVID-19
Transition of role	MIS student	Attention Relevance	Exploring Learning Idea testing	System thinking Real case analysis Concept proving
	IT professional	Confidence Satisfaction	Prototyping Deploying Pilot testing	Workable solution Scenario realization Problem solving
	IT professional facing COVID-19	Volition Reflection	Developing Innovating Refining	Infrastructure support Agile servicing Rapid integration

Smart Technology-Empowered Education and Learning (STEEL)

Smart Technology-Empowered Practice and Servicing (STEPS)

Figure 6   Facilitating the transition

In Figure 6, we have adopted metaphors again by using the terms "steel" and "steps".

5.6 Constructing the Grounded Theory

The students' perceptions of MIS education, IT professional, and COVID-19 outbreaks lead us to the reflections about how to learn, work, adapt, and sustain facing COVID-19 outbreaks through the utilization of smart technologies. The above discussion illustrated that the real power of smart technologies lies in its hidden yet profound role in facilitating the transition of lives facing uncertain situations.

To summarize the discussion, the following grounded theories are proposed.

Grounded theory 1:
The learning in MIS education and the practice of IT professionals can contribute to the realization of smart technology-empowered transition.

Grounded theory 2:

Smart technology-empowered transition can mitigate the impacts of COVID-19 outbreaks and stimulate the cultivation of sustainable societies.

6. Implications

6.1 Implications for MIS Educators and Researchers

MIS students perceive MIS education as an adaptable incubator. This implies they are aware of the fast changing pace of the IT field and the multi-discipline nature of management. They understand the importance of continuous learning for knowledge upgrade. The content of the education needs to be adaptable to environment changes and contingent situations. MIS education is to prepare the students toward caring intellectuals of IT and management.

The outbreak of COVID-19 incurs public uncertainty, pervasive anxiety, and lifestyle disruption.

These disastrous effects will last for years. However, the pandemic also invoked great attention from IT related academics and stimulate reflective thinking of MIS researchers. As the relevance between COVID-19 outbreak and MIS education programs increases, the pandemic situations will expand the knowledge domain and research area of MIS. Case studies and scenario analyses are a starting point for MIS students. The analytics of social pandemic big data is a topic combining theory and application (Bossé & Solaiman, 2018). In particular, the students are aware of the concepts of ethics and social responsibility. They expressed their volition to help with the resolution of the situation. Therefore, MIS educators may consider enhancing the discussion of topics such as big data with uncertainty (Bossé & Solaiman, 2018; Hariri, Fredericks, & Bowers, 2019), social transition (O. Haimson, 2018; O. L. Haimson et al., 2021), and disruption management

(Giuntella, Hyde, Saccardo, & Sadoff, 2021; Zheng, Shou, & Yang, 2021).

Furthermore, all of the interviewees expressed positive experiences about distance education and digital library, despite some of them were forced to use these technologies because of the COVID-19 outbreak. Learning in the clouds is a popular trend of continuous learning. Smart technology-empowered learning enables the generation of adaptable content of education (Marinova et al., 2017). Therefore, learning and education using smart technologies are critical for MIS education since these topics highlight the two equally important facets of MIS education: learning for smart technologies and learning by smart technologies.

6.2 Implications for IT Professionals and managers

Our results indicated that MIS students perceive IT professional as an agile integrator. In the interview dialogues IT professionals are perceived as enablers of digital infrastructure. On top of this infrastructure, they can efficiently develop and deploy various services used by government units, manufacturers, retailers, healthcare providers, and the other sectors. They are the integrators of innovative technologies for corporate and personal users. The practice and experience of IT professionals are valuable reference models of careers for MIS students. Moreover, in recent years various industry sectors are gradually upgrading into new paradigms, such as Industry 4.0 for manufacturing, Fintech for finance, smart healthcare, smart retail, and smart tourism, among others. These industrial upgrades require the services of IT professionals to provide smart technology-empowered solutions. However, the outbreak of COVID-19 presents an unforeseen challenge to all of these industries.

For IT professionals and managers, COVID-19 outbreak provides alerting reflection on IT community. Whenever there is an ecological, economical, or social catastrophe, digital infrastructure becomes a critical supportive resource to continue human activities. The future practices of IT will need to strengthen competences in contingency handling, disaster prevention and mitigation (Ardito, Coccia, & Messeni Petruzzelli, 2021; Bundy, Pfarrer, Short, & Coombs, 2017; Reuter, Hughes, & Kaufhold, 2018), change management, and critical digital infrastructure protection. Moreover, since IT-enabled remote collaboration will be the frequent working mode under pandemic situations, IT professionals also need to develop efficient mechanisms for productive collaboration.

Furthermore, as other industries are using smart technologies and integrated solutions provided by IT professionals to upgrade and evolve, the industry of IT professionals itself will also need to keep up and take the lead. By following the advocacy of Industry 4.0 for the manufacturing industry, the information service industry can also think of the vision and action plan of

"Information Service 4.0" with the empowerment of smart technologies. "Smart technology-empowered information service" and "information service for smart applications" are thus a legitimate ambidextrous development strategy for IT professionals. With a substantial MIS education as a foundation and sustained progress with smart technologies, IT professionals can continue to play the indispensable supportive role for the world.

7. Conclusions

Our goal is to investigate how MIS students perceive the meanings and connections among their MIS education, IT professionals, and COVID-19 confrontation. A cohesive linkage among theoretical knowledge, technical skills, professional competencies, and situational problem solving is critical for MIS students' success in future careers, especially in this unusual time of disastrous pandemic. Providing quality transition paths of practice and experience for MIS students is vital to the development of commitment and competent IT professionals facing real world challenges. We hope these findings will not only help MIS educators fully understand the educational effectiveness of current MIS education programs, but also provide recommendations for managers of organizations in their efforts to recruit and train newly graduated IT workforce.

This study reported meaningful implications regarding MIS students' perceptions of MIS education, IT professional, and COVID-19 outbreak. However, the validity of an argument cannot be firmly established on the basis of a single qualitative study. Further studies on this topic with various research methods and samples are recommended. Such research will help accumulating more empirical evidence for assessing and validating the propositions of this study.

References

Agarwal, N., & Brem, A. (2015). Strategic business transformation through technology convergence: implications from General Electrics industrial internet initiative. *International Journal of Technology Management, 67*(2/3/4), 196-214.

Ardito, L., Coccia, M., & Messeni Petruzzelli, A. (2021). Technological exaptation and crisis management: Evidence from COVID-19 outbreaks. *R&D Management,* 10.1111/radm.12455. doi:10.1111/radm.12455

Atzori, L., Iera, A., & Morabito, G. (2010). The Internet of Things: A survey. *Computer Networks, 54*(15), 2787-2805. doi:10.1016/j.comnet.2010.05.010

Borgia, E. (2014). The Internet of Things vision: Key features, applications and open issues. *Computer Communications, 54,* 1-31. doi:10.1016/j.comcom.2014.09.008

Bossé, É., & Solaiman, B. (2018). Fusion of information and analytics: a discussion on potential methods to cope with uncertainty in complex environments (big data and IoT). *International Journal of Digital Signals and Smart Systems, 2*(4), 279-316.

Bradley, D., Russell, D., Ferguson, I., Isaacs, J., MacLeod, A., & White, R. (2015). The Internet of Things – The future or the end of mechatronics. *Mechatronics, 27*, 57-74. doi:10.1016/j.mechatronics.2015.02.005

Bundy, J., Pfarrer, M. D., Short, C. E., & Coombs, W. T. (2017). Crises and crisis management: Integration, interpretation, and research development. *Journal of management, 43*(6), 1661-1692.

Chang, Y.-S., Hu, K.-J., Chiang, C.-W., & Lugmayr, A. (2020). Applying Mobile Augmented Reality (AR) to Teach Interior Design Students in Layout Plans: Evaluation of Learning Effectiveness Based on the ARCS Model of Learning Motivation Theory.

Sensors, 20(1), 105. Retrieved from https://www.mdpi.com/1424-8220/20/1/105

Corbin, J., & Strauss, A. (1990). Grounded theory research: Procedures, canons, and evaluative criteria. *Qualitative Sociology 19*(6), 418-427.

Dwivedi, Y. K., Hughes, D. L., Coombs, C., Constantiou, I., Duan, Y., Edwards, J. S., ... Upadhyay, N. (2020). Impact of COVID-19 pandemic on information management research and practice: Transforming education, work and life. *International Journal of Information Management, 55*, 102211. doi:https://doi.org/10.1016/j.ijinfomgt.2020.102211

Giuntella, O., Hyde, K., Saccardo, S., & Sadoff, S. (2021). Lifestyle and mental health disruptions during COVID-19. *Proceedings of the National Academy of Sciences, 118*(9).

Gong, M., Liu, L., Sun, X., Yang, Y., Wang, S., & Zhu, H. (2020). Cloud-Based System for Effective Surveillance and Control of COVID-19: Useful

Experiences From Hubei, China. *Journal of Medical Internet Research, 22*(4), e18948. doi:10.2196/18948

Gubbi, J., Buyya, R., Marusic, S., & Palaniswami, M. (2013). Internet of Things (IoT): A vision, architectural elements, and future directions. *Future Generation Computer Systems, 29*(7), 1645-1660. doi:10.1016/j.future.2013.01.010

Haimson, O. (2018). Social Media as Social Transition Machinery. *Proceedings of the ACM on Human-Computer Interaction, 2*(CSCW), 1-21. doi:10.1145/3274332

Haimson, O. L., Carter, A. J., Corvite, S., Wheeler, B., Wang, L., Liu, T., & Lige, A. (2021). The major life events taxonomy: Social readjustment, social media information sharing, and online network separation during times of life transition. *Journal of the Association for Information Science and Technology.*

Hariri, R. H., Fredericks, E. M., & Bowers, K. M. (2019).

Uncertainty in big data analytics: survey, opportunities, and challenges. *Journal of Big Data, 6*(1), 1-16.

Keller, J. M. (2016). Motivation, learning, and technology: Applying the ARCS-V motivation model. *Participatory Educational Research, 3*(2), 1-15.

Kjerkol, I., Linset, K., & Westeren, K. I. (2021). Effects of COVID-19 on communication, services, and life situation for older persons receiving municipal health and care services in Stjørdal municipality in Norway. *Human Behavior and Emerging Technologies, 3*(1), 204-217.

Krotov, V. (2017). The Internet of Things and new business opportunities. *Business Horizons, 60*(6), 831-841. doi:https://doi.org/10.1016/j.bushor.2017.07.009

Marinova, D., de Ruyter, K., Huang, M.-H., Meuter, M. L., & Challagalla, G. (2017). Getting smart:

Learning from technology-empowered frontline interactions. *Journal of Service Research, 20*(1), 29-42.

Miorandi, D., Sicari, S., De Pellegrini, F., & Chlamtac, I. (2012). Internet of things: Vision, applications and research challenges. *Ad Hoc Networks, 10*(7), 1497-1516. doi:10.1016/j.adhoc.2012.02.016

Pflügler, C., Wiesche, M., Becker, N., & Krcmar, H. (2018). Strategies for Retaining Key IT Professionals. *MIS Quarterly Executive, 17*(4), 297-314. Retrieved from http://search.ebscohost.com/login.aspx?direct=true&db=bth&AN=133445204&lang=zh-tw&site=ehost-live

Porter, M. E., & Heppelmann, J. E. (2015). How smart, connected products are transforming companies. *Harvard Business Review, 93*(10), 96-16. Retrieved from http://search.ebscohost.com/login.aspx?direct=true

&db=bth&AN=109338341&lang=zh-tw&site=ehost-live

Reuter, C., Hughes, A. L., & Kaufhold, M.-A. (2018). Social Media in Crisis Management: An Evaluation and Analysis of Crisis Informatics Research. *International Journal of Human–Computer Interaction, 34*(4), 280-294. doi:10.1080/10447318.2018.1427832

Taylor, C., & Dewsbury, B. M. (2018). On the Problem and Promise of Metaphor Use in Science and Science Communication. *Journal of Microbiology and Biology Education, 19*(1), 19.11.46. doi:10.1128/jmbe.v19i1.1538

Thibodeau, P. H., Hendricks, R. K., & Boroditsky, L. (2017). How linguistic metaphor scaffolds reasoning. *Trends in cognitive sciences, 21*(11), 852-863.

Tuli, S., Tuli, S., Tuli, R., & Gill, S. S. (2020). Predicting the growth and trend of COVID-19 pandemic using machine learning and cloud computing. *Internet of Things, 11*, 100222-100222. doi:10.1016/j.iot.2020.100222

Weng, W. H. (2021a). Effect of Internet of Things on Marketing Intelligence and Business Strategy: An Organizational Capability Perspective. *International Journal of Electronic Commerce Studies, 12*(2). doi:10.7903/ijecs.1906

Weng, W. H. (2021b, 28-30 May 2021). *Influential Components for the Sustainability of IoT-enabled Smart Systems: A Hierarchical Analysis.* Paper presented at the 2021 IEEE 3rd Eurasia Conference on Biomedical Engineering, Healthcare and Sustainability (ECBIOS).

Weng, W. H. (2021c). *Prioritizing critical cloud services for disastrous pandemics: A media richness perspective.* Paper presented at the Proceedings of the Twenty-First International Conference on Electronic Business (ICEB 2021), Nanjing, China.

Weng, W. H. (2022). Impact of Competitive Strategy on Big Data Analytics Adoption: An Information Processing Perspective. *International Journal of Electronic Commerce Studies, 13*(2), 1-26. doi:10.7903/ijecs.2013

Weng, W. H., & Lin, W. T. (2014a). *Development assessment and strategy planning in mobile computing industry.* Paper presented at the 2014 IEEE International Conference on Management of Innovation and Technology, Singapore.

Weng, W. H., & Lin, W. T. (2014b). Development trends and strategy planning in big data industry. *Contemporary Management Research, 10*(3).

Whitelaw, S., Mamas, M. A., Topol, E., & Van Spall, H. G. C. (2020). Applications of digital technology in COVID-19 pandemic planning and response. *The Lancet Digital Health, 2*(8), e435-e440. doi:https://doi.org/10.1016/S2589-7500(20)30142-4

Yoo, Y., Henfridsson, O., & Lyytinen, K. (2010). Research Commentary—The New Organizing Logic of Digital Innovation: An Agenda for Information Systems Research. *Information systems research, 21*(4), 724-735. doi:10.1287/isre.1100.0322

Zheng, R., Shou, B., & Yang, J. (2021). Supply disruption management under consumer panic buying and social learning effects. *Omega, 101*, 102238.

Sustainable Systems

Development and Learning

Author: Winston W. H. Weng

Publisher: Winston W. H. Weng

Edition: English eBook edition

Publication Date: December 2024

Copyright © 2024 by Winston W. H. Weng

All Rights Reserved

www.ingramcontent.com/pod-product-compliance
Lightning Source LLC
Chambersburg PA
CBHW071025240526
45469CB00006BD/2088